THIRD EDITION

4A

Skills for Success
READING AND WRITING

Debra Daise | Charl Norloff

OXFORD
UNIVERSITY PRESS

198 Madison Avenue
New York, NY 10016 USA

Great Clarendon Street, Oxford, OX2 6DP, United Kingdom

Oxford University Press is a department of the University of Oxford.
It furthers the University's objective of excellence in research, scholarship,
and education by publishing worldwide. Oxford is a registered trade
mark of Oxford University Press in the UK and in certain other countries

First published in 2020

2024 2023 2022 2021 2020

10 9 8 7 6 5 4 3 2 1

No unauthorized photocopying

ISBN: 978 0 19 490407 0   Student Book 4A with iQ Online pack
ISBN: 978 0 19 490377 6   Student Book 4A as pack component
ISBN: 978 0 19 490431 5   iQ Online student website

Printed in China

This book is printed on paper from certified and well-managed sources

ACKNOWLEDGMENTS

Back cover photograph: Oxford University Press building/David Fisher

Illustrations by: 5W Infographics p.215; Mark Duffin pp.95–96, 103.

*The Publishers would like to thank the following for their kind permission to
reproduce photographs and other copyright material*: 123rf: pp.103 (desert
plant/Oleksandr Petrunovskyi), 125 (woman shopping/Antonio Diaz),
131 (berry cheesecake/rawpixel), 134 (scientist with test tubes/scanrail),
144 (feet on scales/George Tsartsianidis), 181 (graduation ceremony/
dolgachov); Alamy: pp.14 (girl drinking water/Jake Lyell), 17 (meals
on wheel volunteer/Tina Manley), 18 (free meal event/roger parkes),
21 (runner crossing finishing line/Hero Images Inc.), 23 (goals notepad/
ALLASH), 31 (school in India/ephotocorp), 41 (leaving feedback rating/
Anna Berkut), 62 (students bowing to parents/Xinhua), 78 (child walking
off baseball field/Juice Images), 83 (cup and saucer/Nick Young), 88 (empty
wallet/Chris Pancewicz), 107 (irrigation channel Africa/Mike Goldwater),
113 (Otto Lilienthal/INTERFOTO), (Wright brothers/World History
Archive), 126 (schoolchildren on allotment/Paula Solloway), 152 (students
in computer class/imageBROKER), 182 (wildlife on coral reef/SeaTops),
185 (coldwater coral/Frank Hecker), 194–195 (Bristol Bay scenic/Design Pics
Inc), 205 (underwater submersible/david gregs), 236 (reservoir dam/Dimitar
Todorov); AP: p.92 (girl using i-limb/Patrick Record); Getty: pp.cover (close-
up of Crassulaceae plants/Johner Images), 6 (father constructing camp fire/
Hero Images), 12 (community house building project/AFP Contributor),
32 (teen passing advertising hoarding/SOPA Images), 35 (generation z/Tara
Moore), 43 (boy on phone/Eternity in an Instant), 55 (weekend warrior/
Elli Thor Magnusson), 61 (Times Square/Jack Berman), 66 (students
checking noticeboard/Hero Images), 74 (father and daughter fishing/Hero
Images), 91 (group of girls walking/Klaus Vedfelt), 121 (man blowing into
respiratory machine/The AGE), 122 (germinating seeds/LOIC VENANCE),
137 (colorful food/Maximilian Stock Ltd.), 151 (cubed ingredients/Martin
Kreppel/EyeEm), 163 (businessman/Hero Images), 168 (people in art gallery/
JGI/Tom Grill), 169 (analyzing graphs/Wutthichai Luemuang/EyeEm),
(analyst discussing graphs/Ariel Skelley), 175 (woman looking at notice
board/Hero Images), 176 (woman shaking hand/laflor), 178 (decision
tick boxes/jayk7), 193 (salmon fisherman/Jeff Rotman), 206 (urban park/
Vicki Jauron, Babylon and Beyond Photography), 211 (cruise shop on
ocean/Daniel Piraino/EyeEm), 212 (constructing bridge/Construction
Photography/Avalon), 230 (Chernobyl nuclear power station/Wojtek
Laski), 233 (students working together/Westend61), 242 (aerial view of
roads/anucha sirivisansuwan); Oxford University Press: pp.73 (sunset
over sea/Shutterstock; S–F), 108 (clouds/Galyna Andrushko/shutterstock.
com), 146 (citrus fruits/Shutterstock/Studio Dagdagaz), 199 (wind farm/
Shutterstock); Shutterstock: pp.2 (firefighter/Tithi Luadthong), 48 (data
mining/Paul Fleet), 52 (interior of restaurant/Koksharov Dmitry), 58 (female
influencer taking selfie/mentatdgt), 72 (alarm clock/MK photograp.55),
115 (petri dish with mold/grebcha), 139 (pill containing food/Lightspring),
141 (science museum/cowardlion), 142 (lazy man/txking), 155 (frustrated
employee/fizkes), 186 (map of Zealandia/Crystal Eye Studio), 225 (engineer
and apprentices/goodluz); Third party: p.44 (laptop with note/emc design).

*The authors and publisher are grateful to those who have given permission to
reproduce the following extracts and adaptations of copyright material*: p.12
Excerpt from Interview with Katrina fried, author of Everyday Heroes:
50 Americans Changing the World One Nonprofit at a Time. Copyright
© 2012 Katrina Fried, Published by Welcome Books. p.35 Adapted extract
from 'Your Guide to Generation Z: The Frugal, Brand-Wary, Determined
Anti-Millennials' by Elizabeth Segran, 8 September 2016. Used with
permission of Fast Company Copyright © 2018. All rights reserved. p.43
Adapted extract from 'This is why you're addicted to your phone' by Nick
Arnold, 12 October 2017, www.bbc.co.uk. © 2019 BBC. Reproduced by
permission. p.73 Adapted extract from '10 Life Lessons I Learned from
my Dad in 23 years' by Katie Hurley, 10 June 2014, www.huffingtonpost.
com. Reproduced by permission of Katie Hurley, LCSW, author of No
More Mean Girls and The Happy Kid Handbook. p.95 Adapted extract
from 'Five Innovative Technologies That Bring Energy to the Developing
World' by Joseph Stromberg, 2 May 2013, www.smithsonian.com. © 2019
Smithsonian Institution. Reprinted with permission from Smithsonian
Enterprises. All rights reserved. Reproduction in any medium is strictly
prohibited without permission from Smithsonian Institution. p.103
Adapted extract from 'This Device Pulls Water Out of Desert Air' by Emily
Matchar, 20 June 2018, www.smithsonian.com. © 2019 Smithsonian
Institution. Reprinted with permission from Smithsonian Enterprises. All
rights reserved. Reproduction in any medium is strictly prohibited without
permission from Smithsonian Institution. p.134 From 'A Personalized
Nutrition Company Will Use Your DNA To Tell You What To Eat' by Claire
Maldarelli, 25 October 2016, popularscience.com. Used with permission
of PopularScience.com. Copyright © 2018. All rights reserved. p.163
From 'Making My First Post-College Decision' by Devin Reams, www.
employeeevolution.com. Reproduced by permission. p.194 Extract from
'Is Alaska's Pebble Mine the Next Keystone XL?' by Svati Kirsten Narula, 14
March 2014, www.theatlantic.com. © Svati Kirsten Narula. Reproduced by
permission. p.224 Adapted extract from 'How to … design a student project
that benefits the developing world' by Keith Pullen, 24 January 2014,
www.theguardian.com. © Copyright Guardian News & Media Ltd 2018.
Reprinted by permission.

ACKNOWLEDGMENTS

We would like to acknowledge the teachers from all over the world who participated in the development process and review of *Q: Skills for Success* Third Edition.

USA

Kate Austin, Avila University, MO; **Sydney Bassett**, Auburn Global University, AL; **Michael Beamer**, USC, CA; **Renae Betten**, CBU, CA; **Pepper Boyer**, Auburn Global University, AL; **Marina Broeder**, Mission College, CA; **Thomas Brynmore**, Auburn Global University, AL; **Britta Burton**, Mission College, CA; **Kathleen Castello**, Mission College, CA; **Teresa Cheung**, North Shore Community College, MA; **Shantall Colebrooke**, Auburn Global University, AL; **Kyle Cooper**, Troy University, AL; **Elizabeth Cox**, Auburn Global University, AL; **Ashley Ekers**, Auburn Global University, AL; **Rhonda Farley**, Los Rios Community College, CA; **Marcus Frame**, Troy University, AL; **Lora Glaser**, Mission College, CA; **Hala Hamka**, Henry Ford College, MI; **Shelley A. Harrington**, Henry Ford College, MI; **Barrett J. Heusch**, Troy University, AL; **Beth Hill**, St. Charles Community College, MO; **Patty Jones**, Troy University, AL; **Tom Justice**, North Shore Community College, MA; **Robert Klein**, Troy University, AL; **Patrick Maestas**, Auburn Global University, AL; **Elizabeth Merchant**, Auburn Global University, AL; **Rosemary Miketa**, Henry Ford College, MI; **Myo Myint**, Mission College, CA; **Lance Noe**, Troy University, AL; **Irene Pannatier**, Auburn Global University, AL; **Annie Percy**, Troy University, AL; **Erin Robinson**, Troy University, AL; **Juliane Rosner**, Mission College, CA; **Mary Stevens**, North Shore Community College, MA; **Pamela Stewart**, Henry Ford College, MI; **Karen Tucker**, Georgia Tech, GA; **Loreley Wheeler**, North Shore Community College, MA; **Amanda Wilcox**, Auburn Global University, AL; **Heike Williams**, Auburn Global University, AL

Canada

Angelika Brunel, Collège Ahuntsic, QC; **David Butler**, English Language Institute, BC; **Paul Edwards**, Kwantlen Polytechnic University, BC; **Cody Hawver**, University of British Columbia, BC; **Olivera Jovovic**, Kwantlen Polytechnic University, BC; **Tami Moffatt**, University of British Columbia, BC; **Dana Pynn**, Vancouver Island University, BC

Latin America

Georgette Barreda, SENATI, Peru; **Claudia Cecilia Díaz Romero**, Colegio América, Mexico; **Jeferson Ferro**, Uninter, Brazil; **Mayda Hernández**, English Center, Mexico; **Jose Ixtaccihusatl**, Instituto Tecnológico de Tecomatlán, Mexico; **Andreas Paulus Pabst**, CBA Idiomas, Brazil; **Amanda Carla Pas**, Instituição de Ensino Santa Izildinha, Brazil; **Allen Quesada Pacheco**, University of Costa Rica, Costa Rica; **Rolando Sánchez**, Escuela Normal de Tecámac, Mexico; **Luis Vasquez**, CESNO, Mexico

Asia

Asami Atsuko, Women's University, Japan; **Rene Bouchard**, Chinzei Keiai Gakuen, Japan; **Francis Brannen**, Sangmyung University, South Korea; **Haeyun Cho**, Sogang University, South Korea; **Daniel Craig**, Sangmyung University, South Korea; **Thomas Cuming**, Royal Melbourne Institute of Technology, Vietnam; **Jissen Joshi Daigaku**, Women's University, Japan; **Nguyen Duc Dat**, OISP, Vietnam; **Wayne Devitte**, Tokai University, Japan; **James D. Dunn**, Tokai University, Japan; **Fergus Hann**, Tokai University, Japan; **Michael Hood**, Nihon University College of Commerce, Japan; **Hideyuki Kashimoto**, Shijonawate High School, Japan; **David Kennedy**, Nihon University, Japan; **Anna Youngna Kim**, Sogang University, South Korea; **Jae Phil Kim**, Sogang University, South Korea; **Jaganathan Krishnasamy**, GB Academy, Malaysia; **Peter Laver**, Incheon National University, South Korea; **Hung Hoang Le**, Ho Chi Minh City University of Technology, Vietnam; **Hyon Sook Lee**, Sogang University, South Korea; **Ji-seon Lee**, Iruda English Institute, South Korea; **Joo Young Lee**, Sogang University, South Korea; **Phung Tu Luc**, Ho Chi Minh City University of Technology, Vietnam; **Richard Mansbridge**, Hoa Sen University, Vietnam; **Kahoko Matsumoto**, Tokai University, Japan; **Elizabeth May**, Sangmyung University, South Korea; **Naoyuki Naganuma**, Tokai University, Japan;

Hiroko Nishikage, Taisho University, Japan; **Yongjun Park**, Sangji University, South Korea; **Paul Rogers**, Dongguk University, South Korea; **Scott Schafer**, Inha University, South Korea; **Michael Schvaudner**, Tokai University, Japan; **Brendan Smith**, RMIT University, School of Languages and English, Vietnam; **Peter Snashall**, Huachiew Chalermprakiet University, Thailand; Makoto Takeda, Sendai Third Senior High School, Japan; **Peter Talley**, Mahidol University, Faculty of ICT, Thailand; **Byron Thigpen**, Sogang University, South Korea; **Junko Yamaai**, Tokai University, Japan; **Junji Yamada**, Taisho University, Japan; **Sayoko Yamashita**, Women's University, Japan; **Masami Yukimori**, Taisho University, Japan

Middle East and North Africa

Sajjad Ahmad, Taibah University, Saudi Arabia; **Basma Alansari**, Taibah University, Saudi Arabia; **Marwa Al-ashqar**, Taibah University, Saudi Arabia; **Dr. Rashid Al-Khawaldeh**, Taibah University, Saudi Arabia; **Mohamed Almohamed**, Taibah University, Saudi Arabia; **Dr Musaad Alrahaili**, Taibah University, Saudi Arabia; **Hala Al Sammar**, Kuwait University, Kuwait; **Ahmed Alshammari**, Taibah University, Saudi Arabia; **Ahmed Alshamy**, Taibah University, Saudi Arabia; **Doniazad sultan AlShraideh**, Taibah University, Saudi Arabia; **Sahar Amer**, Taibah University, Saudi Arabia; **Nabeela Azam**, Taibah University, Saudi Arabia; **Hassan Bashir**, Edex, Saudi Arabia; **Rachel Batchilder**, College of the North Atlantic, Qatar; **Nicole Cuddie**, Community College of Qatar, Qatar; **Mahdi Duris**, King Saud University, Saudi Arabia; **Ahmed Ege**, Institute of Public Administration, Saudi Arabia; **Magda Fadle**, Victoria College, Egypt; **Mohammed Hassan**, Taibah University, Saudi Arabia; **Tom Hodgson**, Community College of Qatar, Qatar; **Ayub Agbar Khan**, Taibah University, Saudi Arabia; **Cynthia Le Joncour**, Taibah University, Saudi Arabia; **Ruari Alexander MacLeod**, Community College of Qatar, Qatar; **Nasir Mahmood**, Taibah University, Saudi Arabia; **Duria Salih Mahmoud**, Taibah University, Saudi Arabia; **Ameera McKoy**, Taibah University, Saudi Arabia; **Chaker Mhamdi**, Buraimi University College, Oman; **Baraa Shiekh Mohamed**, Community College of Qatar, Qatar; **Abduleelah Mohammed**, Taibah University, Saudi Arabia; **Shumaila Nasir**, Taibah University, Saudi Arabia; **Kevin Onwordi**, Taibah University, Saudi Arabia; **Dr. Navid Rahmani**, Community College of Qatar, Qatar; **Dr. Sabah Salman Sabbah**, Community College of Qatar, Qatar; **Salih**, Taibah University, Saudi Arabia; **Verna Santos-Nafrada**, King Saud University, Saudi Arabia; **Gamal Abdelfattah Shehata**, Taibah University, Saudi Arabia; **Ron Stefan**, Institute of Public Administration, Saudi Arabia; **Dr. Saad Torki**, Imam Abdulrahman Bin Faisal University, Dammam, Saudi Arabia; **Silvia Yafai**, Applied Technology High School/Secondary Technical School, UAE; **Mahmood Zar**, Taibah University, Saudi Arabia; **Thouraya Zheni**, Taibah University, Saudi Arabia

Turkey

Sema Babacan, Istanbul Medipol University; **Bilge Çöllüoğlu Yakar**, Bilkent University; **Liana Corniel**, Koc University; **Savas Geylanioglu**, Izmir Bahcesehir Science and Technology College; **Öznur Güler**, Giresun University; **Selen Bilginer Halefoğlu**, Maltepe University; **Ahmet Konukoğlu**, Hasan Kalyoncu University; **Mehmet Salih Yoğun**, Gaziantep Hasan Kalyoncu University; **Fatih Yücel**, Beykent University

Europe

Amina Al Hashamia, University of Exeter, UK; **Irina Gerasimova**, Saint-Petersburg Mining University, Russia; **Jodi**, Las Dominicas, Spain; **Marina Khanykova**, School 179, Russia; **Oksana Postnikova**, Lingua Practica, Russia; **Nina Vasilchenko**, Soho-Bridge Language School, Russia

CRITICAL THINKING

The unique critical thinking approach of the *Q: Skills for Success* series has been further enhanced in the Third Edition. New features help you analyze, synthesize, and develop your ideas.

Unit question
The thought-provoking unit questions engage you with the topic and provide a critical thinking framework for the unit.

UNIT QUESTION

What makes someone admirable?

A. Discuss these questions with your classmates.

1. Why do we like to read stories about admirable people?
2. Who do you admire? Why do you admire this person?
3. Look at the photo. What makes this person admirable?

Analysis
You can discuss your opinion of each reading text and analyze how it changes your perspective on the unit question.

WRITE WHAT YOU THINK

A. DISCUSS Discuss the questions in a group.

1. Do athletes make good role models? Why or why not?
2. Who are you a role model for?
3. Imagine yourself 20 years from now. What would you like to hear people saying about you? What can you do between now and then so that people will say that?

B. SYNTHESIZE Choose one of the questions from Activity A and write a paragraph of 5–7 sentences in response. Look back at your Quick Write on page 5 as you think about what you learned.

NEW! **Critical Thinking Strategy with video**
Each unit includes a Critical Thinking Strategy with activities to give you step-by-step guidance in critical analysis of texts. An accompanying instructional video (available on iQ Online) provides extra support and examples.

CRITICAL THINKING STRATEGY

Analyzing texts for cause and effect relationships
Some texts clearly describe cause and effect relationships. In other texts, the reader must analyze the information in the text to understand potential cause and effect between the events or elements presented.

An example of this can be found in Reading 1, Exercise F (p. 129). There you completed a chart on the benefits of an urban garden. To do this, you had to analyze the connection between causes and effects to determine whether they are related.

Cause: Food doesn't have to be brought to supermarkets.
Effect: Food is fresher. (Because it doesn't have to go to the supermarket, it can be eaten sooner after it is picked.)

Not an effect: Children learn how to plant and grow vegetables. (This is true for programs aimed toward children, but it is not an effect of food not going to supermarkets. The two are not directly related.)

iQ PRACTICE Go online to watch the Critical Thinking Skill Video and check your comprehension. *Practice > Unit 5 > Activity 6*

NEW! **Bloom's Taxonomy**
Pink activity headings integrate verbs from Bloom's Taxonomy to help you see how each activity develops critical thinking skills.

C. ANALYZE Reread paragraphs 6, 7, and 8 of Reading 1. Consider the causes and the possible effects. Check *yes* (✓) if they are related and *no* (✓) if they are not. Use the information in the article and your own experience. Then compare answers with a partner and give reasons.

1. **Paragraph 6** Cause: shopping at a small local farmers' market instead of a large supermarket

   a. ☐ yes ☐ no Effect: eating fresher food
   b. ☐ yes ☐ no Effect: saving money
   c. ☐ yes ☐ no Effect: sharing a meal with others

2. **Paragraph 7** Cause: learning to cook

   a. ☐ yes ☐ no Effect: improving physical fitness
   b. ☐ yes ☐ no Effect: eating well

THREE TYPES OF VIDEO

UNIT VIDEO

The unit videos include high-interest documentaries and reports on a wide variety of subjects, all linked to the unit topic and question. All videos are from authentic sources.

NEW! "Work with the Video" pages guide you in watching, understanding, and discussing the unit videos. The activities help you see the connection to the Unit Question and the other texts in the unit.

CRITICAL THINKING VIDEO

NEW! Narrated by the Q series authors, these short videos give you further instruction into the Critical Thinking Strategy of each unit using engaging images and graphics. You can use them to get a deeper understanding of the Critical Thinking Strategy.

SKILLS VIDEO

NEW! These instructional videos provide illustrated explanations of skills and grammar points in the Student Book. They can be viewed in class or assigned for a flipped classroom, for homework, or for review. One skill video is available for every unit.

Easily access all videos in the Resources section of iQ Online.

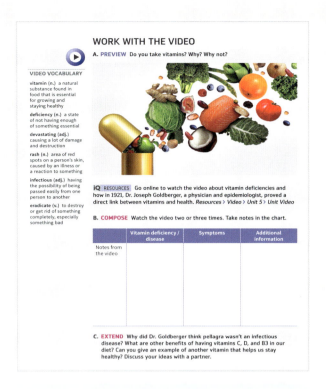

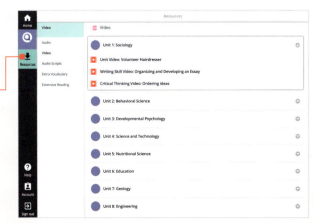

VOCABULARY

A research-based vocabulary program focuses on the words you need to know academically and professionally.

The vocabulary syllabus in *Q: Skills for Success* is correlated to the CEFR (see page 244) and linked to two word lists: the Oxford 5000 and the OPAL (Oxford Phrasal Academic Lexicon).

⋮+ OXFORD 5000

The Oxford 5000 is an expanded core word list for advanced learners of English. As well as the Oxford 3000 core list, the Oxford 5000 includes an additional 2,000 words, guiding learners at B2-C1 level on the most useful high-level words to learn.

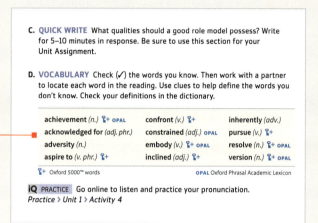

C. QUICK WRITE What qualities should a good role model possess? Write for 5–10 minutes in response. Be sure to use this section for your Unit Assignment.

D. VOCABULARY Check (✓) the words you know. Then work with a partner to locate each word in the reading. Use clues to help define the words you don't know. Check your definitions in the dictionary.

achievement *(n.)* ⋮+ OPAL	confront *(v.)* ⋮+	inherently *(adv.)*
acknowledged for *(adj. phr.)*	constrained *(adj.)* OPAL	pursue *(v.)* ⋮+
adversity *(n.)*	embody *(v.)* ⋮+ OPAL	resolve *(n.)* ⋮+ OPAL
aspire to *(v. phr.)* ⋮+	inclined *(adj.)* ⋮+	version *(n.)* ⋮+ OPAL

⋮+ Oxford 5000™ words   OPAL Oxford Phrasal Academic Lexicon

iQ PRACTICE Go online to listen and practice your pronunciation.
Practice ▸ Unit 1 ▸ Activity 4

Vocabulary Key
In vocabulary activities, ⋮+ shows you the word is in the Oxford 5000 and **OPAL** shows you the word or phrase is in the OPAL.

OPAL
OXFORD PHRASAL ACADEMIC LEXICON

NEW! The OPAL is a collection of four word lists that provide an essential guide to the most important words and phrases to know for academic English. The word lists are based on the Oxford Corpus of Academic English and the British Academic Spoken English corpus. The OPAL includes both spoken and written academic English and both individual words and longer phrases.

Academic Language tips in the Student Book give information about how words and phrases from the OPAL are used and offer help with features such as collocations and phrasal verbs.

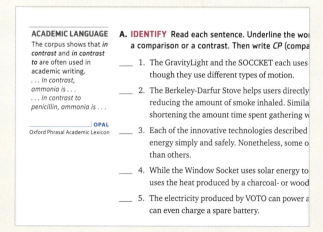

ACADEMIC LANGUAGE
The corpus shows that *in contrast* and *in contrast to* are often used in academic writing.
. . . In contrast, ammonia is . . .
. . . In contrast to penicillin, ammonia is . . .
_____ **OPAL**
Oxford Phrasal Academic Lexicon

A. IDENTIFY Read each sentence. Underline the wo[rd]
a comparison or a contrast. Then write *CP* (compa[rison]

____ 1. The GravityLight and the SOCCKET each uses
though they use different types of motion.

____ 2. The Berkeley-Darfur Stove helps users directly
reducing the amount of smoke inhaled. Simila[r]
shortening the amount time spent gathering w[ood]

____ 3. Each of the innovative technologies described
energy simply and safely. Nonetheless, some o[f]
than others.

____ 4. While the Window Socket uses solar energy to
uses the heat produced by a charcoal- or wood[-]

____ 5. The electricity produced by VOTO can power a
can even charge a spare battery.

EXTENSIVE READING

NEW! Extensive Reading is a program of reading for pleasure at a level that matches your language ability.

There are many benefits to Extensive Reading:

- It helps you to become a better reader in general.
- It helps to increase your reading speed.
- It can improve your reading comprehension.
- It increases your vocabulary range.
- It can improve your grammar and writing skills.
- It's great for motivation—reading something that is interesting for its own sake.

Each unit of *Q: Skills for Success* Third Edition has been aligned to an Oxford Graded Reader based on the appropriate topic and level of language proficiency. The first chapter of each recommended graded reader can be downloaded from iQ Online Resources.

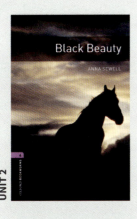

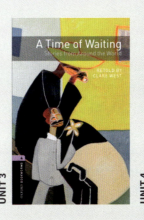

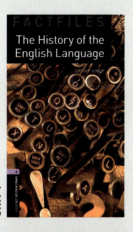

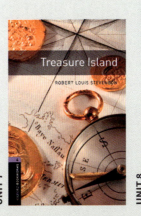

iQ ONLINE extends your learning beyond the classroom.

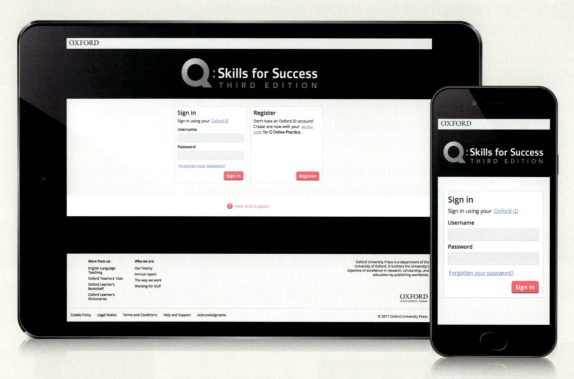

- Practice activities provide essential skills practice and support.
- Automatic grading and progress reports show you what you have mastered and where you still need more practice.
- Discussion Board to discuss the Unit Questions helps you develop your critical thinking.
- Writing Tutor helps you practice your academic writing skills.
- Essential resources such as audio and video are easy to access anytime.

NEW TO THE THIRD EDITION

- Site is optimized for mobile use so you can use it on your phone.
- An updated interface allows easy navigation around the activities, tests, resources, and scores.
- New Critical Thinking Videos expand on the Critical Thinking Strategies in the Student Book.
- Extensive Reading program helps you improve your vocabulary and reading skills.

How to use iQ ONLINE

Go to **Practice** to find additional practice and support to complement your learning in the classroom.

Go to **Resources** to find
- All Student Book video
- All Student Book audio
- Critical Thinking videos
- Skills videos
- Extensive Reading

Go to **Messages** and **Discussion Board** to communicate with your teacher and classmates.

Online tests assigned by your teacher help you assess your progress and see where you still need more practice.

Progress bar shows you how many activities you have completed.

View your scores for all activities.

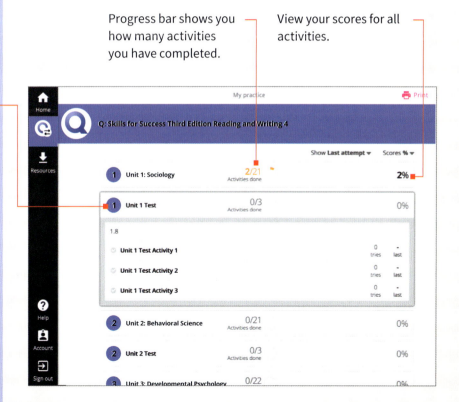

AUTHORS AND CONSULTANTS

AUTHORS

Debra Daise teaches at the University of North Carolina at Charlotte after many years of teaching in Colorado. She has long been interested in helping students develop a love for reading and writing.

Charl Norloff taught ESL at the University of Colorado for 30 years. Prior to that, she taught EFL in the Middle East. She has a special interest in teaching reading and writing to help students prepare for academic success.

SERIES CONSULTANTS

Lawrence J. Zwier holds an M.A. in TESL from the University of Minnesota. He is currently the Associate Director for Curriculum Development at the English Language Center at Michigan State University in East Lansing. He has taught ESL/EFL in the United States, Saudi Arabia, Malaysia, Japan, and Singapore.

Marguerite Ann Snow holds a Ph.D. in Applied Linguistics from UCLA. She teaches in the TESOL M.A. program in the Charter College of Education at California State University, Los Angeles. She was a Fulbright scholar in Hong Kong and Cyprus. In 2006, she received the President's Distinguished Professor award at CSULA. She has trained ESL teachers in the United States and EFL teachers in more than 25 countries. She is the author/editor of numerous publications in the areas of content-based instruction, English for academic purposes, and standards for English teaching and learning. She is a co-editor of *Teaching English as a Second or Foreign Language* (4th ed.).

CRITICAL THINKING CONSULTANT James Dunn is a Junior Associate Professor at Tokai University and the Coordinator of the JALT Critical Thinking Special Interest Group. His research interests include Critical Thinking skills' impact on student brain function during English learning, as measured by EEG. His educational goals are to help students understand that they are capable of more than they might think and to expand their cultural competence with critical thinking and higher-order thinking skills.

ASSESSMENT CONSULTANT Elaine Boyd has worked in assessment for over 30 years for international testing organizations. She has designed and delivered courses in assessment literacy and is also the author of several EL exam coursebooks for leading publishers. She is an Associate Tutor (M.A. TESOL/Linguistics) at University College, London. Her research interests are classroom assessment, issues in managing feedback, and intercultural competences.

VOCABULARY CONSULTANT Cheryl Boyd Zimmerman is Professor Emeritus at California State University, Fullerton. She specialized in second-language vocabulary acquisition, an area in which she is widely published. She taught graduate courses on second-language acquisition, culture, vocabulary, and the fundamentals of TESOL, and has been a frequent invited speaker on topics related to vocabulary teaching and learning. She is the author of *Word Knowledge: A Vocabulary Teacher's Handbook* and Series Director of *Inside Reading, Inside Writing*, and *Inside Listening and Speaking* published by Oxford University Press.

ONLINE INTEGRATION Chantal Hemmi holds an Ed.D. TEFL and is a Japan-based teacher trainer and curriculum designer. Since leaving her position as Academic Director of the British Council in Tokyo, she has been teaching at the Center for Language Education and Research at Sophia University on an EAP/CLIL program offered for undergraduates. She delivers lectures and teacher trainings throughout Japan, Indonesia, and Malaysia.

COMMUNICATIVE GRAMMAR CONSULTANT Nancy Schoenfeld holds an M.A. in TESOL from Biola University in La Mirada, California, and has been an English language instructor since 2000. She has taught ESL in California and Hawaii, and EFL in Thailand and Kuwait. She has also trained teachers in the United States and Indonesia. Her interests include teaching vocabulary, extensive reading, and student motivation. She is currently an English Language Instructor at Kuwait University.

CONTENTS

Sociology

1

READING   previewing and predicting
VOCABULARY   using the dictionary
WRITING   organizing and developing an essay
CRITICAL THINKING   ordering ideas
GRAMMAR   restrictive relative clauses

What makes someone admirable?

A. Discuss these questions with your classmates.

1. Why do we like to read stories about admirable people?

2. Who do you admire? Why do you admire this person?

3. Look at the photo. What makes this person admirable?

B. Listen to *The Q Classroom* online. Then answer these questions.

1. Marcus says admirable people are brave and sacrifice themselves. What two examples does he give? Yuna says regular people can also be admirable. What example does she give? What do you think makes someone admirable?

2. What qualities of an admirable person do Felix and Sophy discuss? Which qualities are most important, in your opinion?

iQ PRACTICE Go to the online discussion board to discuss the Unit Question with your classmates. *Practice › Unit 1 › Activity 1*

UNIT OBJECTIVE

Read an essay and a newspaper interview. Gather information and ideas to write an analysis essay about what makes someone admirable.

READING 1

We All Need a Role Model

OBJECTIVE ▶ You are going to read an essay about role models. Use the essay to gather information and ideas for your Unit Assignment.

PREVIEW THE READING

READING SKILL Previewing and predicting

When you **preview** a text, you look through it quickly to learn general information. To preview:

- Read the title of the text.

- Look at any charts, graphs, pictures, or captions.

- Skim the text for paragraph headings. These indicate important ideas that will be developed in the text.

Previewing will help you **predict** what the text is about and prepare you to better understand it.

TIP FOR SUCCESS

When you write a research paper, you need to get information from a variety of sources. Previewing many books and articles will help you decide which ones are important for your research.

A. PREVIEW Read the title and look at the picture on page 6. Write two things you think the essay might be about.

1. _____

2. _____

B. IDENTIFY Skim the essay and read the paragraph headings. Then look at the pairs of ideas below. Check (✓) one idea in each pair that you think might be developed in the essay.

1. ☐ the qualities of role models   ☐ a description of a specific role model

2. ☐ how people become role models   ☐ which people may be role models

3. ☐ how role models can inspire us   ☐ how we can inspire others

4. ☐ why role models do wrong things   ☐ how role models learn from mistakes

iQ PRACTICE Go online for more practice with previewing and predicting. *Practice > Unit 1 > Activity 2*

C. QUICK WRITE What qualities should a good role model possess? Write for 5–10 minutes in response. Be sure to use this section for your Unit Assignment.

D. VOCABULARY Check (✓) the words you know. Then work with a partner to locate each word in the reading. Use clues to help define the words you don't know. Check your definitions in the dictionary.

achievement *(n.)* ⚡+ OPAL	confront *(v.)* ⚡+	inherently *(adv.)*
acknowledged for *(adj. phr.)*	constrained *(adj.)* OPAL	pursue *(v.)* ⚡+
adversity *(n.)*	embody *(v.)* ⚡+ OPAL	resolve *(n.)* ⚡+ OPAL
aspire to *(v. phr.)* ⚡+	inclined *(adj.)* ⚡+	version *(n.)* ⚡+ OPAL

⚡+ Oxford 5000™ words   OPAL Oxford Phrasal Academic Lexicon

iQ PRACTICE Go online to listen and practice your pronunciation.
Practice ⟩ Unit 1 ⟩ Activity 4

WORK WITH THE READING

A. INVESTIGATE Read the essay and gather information about what makes someone admirable.

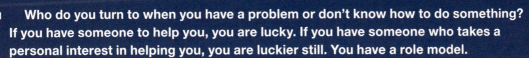

We All Need a Role Model

1   Who do you turn to when you have a problem or don't know how to do something? If you have someone to help you, you are lucky. If you have someone who takes a personal interest in helping you, you are luckier still. You have a role model.

ACADEMIC LANGUAGE
The phrase *not necessarily* is often used in academic writing to express contrast.

──────────| **OPAL**
Oxford Phrasal Academic Lexicon

⭐ Definition of a Role Model

2   Just what is a role model? First, let's recognize what it is not. It is not necessarily the smartest, strongest, or most successful person you know—although it could be. A role model is a person who has the characteristics you want for yourself and who can help you develop those traits. In other words, a role model both **embodies** positive qualities and teaches others directly or through example.

⭐ Who Can Be a Role Model?

3   For most of us, our parents are our first role models. From when we are young children, they help us learn how to interact with other people—how to share, how to ask for what we need, and how to disagree without hurting someone. They are **inherently** interested in us and want us to do well. Furthermore, our parents teach us how to be adults in our society. A mother demonstrates to her daughters how to be a daughter, a woman, a wife, and a

mother. Lessons learned from our parents will stay with us throughout our lives.

4   Other family members also serve as role models. Grandparents, uncles and aunts, cousins, and even siblings can show us how to manage our daily lives. Other obvious candidates include teachers and community leaders.

5   Sometimes we find role models in unexpected places. A family story might inspire us to have the same generosity as our grandfather had. We might see a young child fall, pick herself up, fall again, and pick herself up again. Her **resolve** might inspire us to continue in our own struggles, just as she learns to stand, keep her balance, and take a step. We might even find a model within ourselves, remembering back to a time when we were brave, or imagining a different **version** of ourselves who has the quality we desire.

★ What Role Models Do

6   Besides showing us how to do different things, a good role model also inspires us to **pursue** our dreams and **achievements**. A wise lawyer may inspire one person to study law, while a competent, compassionate physician may lead another person to the medical profession. Role models should empower others to become good parents, leaders, and members of society, and to internalize the qualities that they value. Therefore, role models must do the right thing, even when no one is watching, even when they won't be **acknowledged for** what they have done.

★ When Things Go Wrong

7   It is easy to be a role model when everything is going well, but it is perhaps more important to be a role model when things go wrong. A role model can show us how to handle **adversity**. For instance, we all make mistakes, but what do we do when we realize that we have made one? Do we try to hide it or pretend that it never happened? Are we **inclined** to look for someone to blame? Do we get angry?

8   A role model can show us how to deal with mistakes. A parent or teacher can help us repair any damage that was done or soothe any feelings that were hurt. He or she can listen to us, advise us on alternative courses

A role model shows us how to do different things and how to handle adversity.

of action, and support us as we make amends. The example of a community leader might serve to guide us toward appropriate action, encouraging us to imagine what he would do in our circumstances.

9   Other situations that we might find ourselves in include dealing with stress, illness, or other misfortunes. **Confronting** these predicaments and overcoming them is made easier by the knowledge that people we admire and respect have faced similar conditions. Asking ourselves what they would do might help us be brave for a little while longer or figure out how to deal with life when we feel **constrained** by difficulties.

10   We need role models throughout our lives, and we only need to look around us to find someone who has experienced what we are going through, who has faced difficult decisions, or who has accomplished something we **aspire to** do. Sometimes we only have to look as far as the mirror to see a role model for our children, our neighbors, or even ourselves. Who is your role model? Maybe it is time to say thank you.

B. VOCABULARY Here are some words and phrases from Reading 1. Read the sentences. Then write each bold word next to the correct definition. You may need to change the form of some of the words.

VOCABULARY SKILL REVIEW

Remember to read the whole sentence and consider the *context*. This can help you identify the correct meaning of a word.

1. My father **embodies** the quality of honesty; he never tells a lie.

2. The best athletes have the **resolve** to keep trying even when everything looks hopeless.

3. I will **pursue** my goal to be an engineer even though it will be difficult.

4. Winning the competition was an incredible **achievement** for such a young player.

5. When you set goals, don't be **constrained** by your present situation. If you can dream it, you can do it.

6. The athlete is suffering from a long-term injury, but he still **aspires to** race at the Olympics.

7. Skydiving is an **inherently** dangerous sport.

8. We all want to be **acknowledged for** our good deeds and the things we do to help others.

9. He had a hard life, but the **adversity** and challenges he faced made him a stronger person.

10. She had to **confront** the problem even though she was frightened.

11. I prefer my usual routine and am not **inclined** to try new things.

12. The first witness's **version** of the accident was quite different from what the second witness described.

a. _____ (*adj.*) recognized or shown appreciation for something

b. _____ (*n.*) a strong determination to do something

c. _____ (adv.) being a basic part of something that cannot be removed

d. _____ (v. phr.) to have a strong desire to do or become something

e. _____ (adj.) limited by something or someone

f. _____ (n.) a form of something that is different from another form of the same thing

g. _____ (n.) something that has been done successfully, especially through hard work or skill

h. _____ (v.) to deal with a problem or difficult situation

i. _embody_____ (v.) to represent an idea or quality

j. _____ (adj.) wanting to do something

k. _____ (n.) a difficult or unpleasant situation

l. _____ (v.) to try to achieve something over a period of time

iQ PRACTICE Go online for more practice with the vocabulary.
Practice > Unit 1 > Activity 5

C. RESTATE Answer these questions.

1. What is the main idea of the essay? Write it in a complete sentence.

_____

2. The main idea is found in two places. Where did you find the main idea?

_____

D. IDENTIFY Read the sentences. Number the main ideas in the order they are developed in the essay. (Use the headings in the essay to help you.)

____ a. Role models can show us how to deal with mistakes.

____ b. Role models can show us how to deal with problems.

_1_ c. A role model is a person with qualities that other people want to have.

____ d. Role models inspire us to develop our talents and abilities.

____ e. Many different kinds of people are role models.

E. EXPLAIN Answer these questions.

1. Who are some of the people that can be role models? _____

_____

2. How can a lawyer or doctor serve as a role model? _____

_____

3. How can a role model help us deal with mistakes? _____

_____

_____

4. When is another time role models might help us? _____

_____

_____

F. CATEGORIZE Read the statements. Write *T* (true) or *F* (false) and the paragraph number where the answer is found. Then correct each false statement to make it true according to the essay.

____ 1. A role model is sometimes the most successful person you know. (paragraph ____)

_____

____ 2. A teacher is usually our first role model. (paragraph ____)

_____

____ 3. A young child can be a role model. (paragraph ____)

_____

____ 4. You can be your own role model. (paragraph ____)

_____

____ 5. A role model is supposed to do the right thing. (paragraph ____)

_____

____ 6. A role model never makes mistakes. (paragraph ____)

_____

____ 7. We need role models only when we confront adversity. (paragraph ____)

_____

____ 8. It's hard to find a role model. (paragraph ____)

_____

G. CATEGORIZE Complete the chart with two more people the essay identified as role models and what they can teach us.

Role models	What they can teach us

1. parents	1. how to interact with other people:
	    -how to share
	    -how to ask for what we need
	    -how to disagree without hurting someone
	2. how to be adults in our society

2.	
3.	

H. SYNTHESIZE Look back at your Quick Write on page 5. What qualities should a good role model possess? Add any new ideas or information you learned from the reading.

iQ PRACTICE   Go online for additional reading and comprehension.
Practice > Unit 1 > Activity 3

WRITE WHAT YOU THINK

A. DISCUSS Discuss the questions in a group.

1. Do athletes make good role models? Why or why not?

2. Who are you a role model for?

3. Imagine yourself 20 years from now. What would you like to hear people saying about you? What can you do between now and then so that people will say that?

B. SYNTHESIZE Choose one of the questions from Activity A and write a paragraph of 5–7 sentences in response. Look back at your Quick Write on page 5 as you think about what you learned.

Everyday Heroes

You are going to read an interview with Katrina Fried, the author of *Everyday Heroes: 50 Americans Changing the World One Nonprofit at a Time*. Use the interview to gather information and ideas for your Unit Assignment.

PREVIEW THE READING

A. PREVIEW Answer the questions.

1. Read the title of the article and skim the first three paragraphs. Which of the two definitions is better for the title "Everyday Heroes"?

   a. special people who are heroes all the time

   b. common, normal people who do something special with their lives

   What information from the article helped you find the answer?

   _____

2. Read the question that comes before paragraph 4. What are two answers to that question? Where did you find the answers?

   _____

   _____

3. There are many people's names in the interview, such as Roger Egger, Rebecca Onie, and Adam Braun. Why are these people named in the interview?

   _____

B. QUICK WRITE If you could do something to make your community better, what would you do? What would you need in order to accomplish this? Write for 5–10 minutes in response. Be sure to use this section for your Unit Assignment.

C. VOCABULARY Check (✓) the words you know. Use a dictionary to define any new or unknown words. Then discuss with a partner how the words will relate to the unit.

advocate *(n.)* 🔑+	**empower** *(v.)* 🔑+ OPAL	**humility** *(n.)*
authenticity *(n.)*	**exponential** *(adj.)*	**perceive** *(v.)* 🔑+ OPAL
cause *(n.)* 🔑+ OPAL	**funding** *(n.)* 🔑+ OPAL	**personify** *(v.)*
diverse *(adj.)* 🔑+ OPAL	**humanitarian** *(adj.)* 🔑+	**phenomenon** *(n.)* 🔑+ OPAL

🔑+ Oxford 5000™ words   **OPAL** Oxford Phrasal Academic Lexicon

iQ PRACTICE Go online to listen and practice your pronunciation.
Practice ⟩ Unit 1 ⟩ Activity 6

WORK WITH THE READING

 A. INVESTIGATE Read the interview and gather information about what makes someone admirable.

EVERYDAY HEROES
AN INTERVIEW WITH WRITER KATRINA FRIED

Q: *What makes an everyday hero?*

1 **A:** In this book, "everyday heroes" are not those that **personify** physical bravery. Though heroes such as firefighters are by no means less praiseworthy, I chose to feature passionate promoters of social justice and equality. Their work is **humanitarian** in nature. They are founders or leaders of successful nonprofits[1], representing a **diverse** range of **causes** and people. Nearly all self-identify as social entrepreneurs[2].

Q: *Some readers might perceive a contradiction in the phrase "everyday heroes." Is heroism an everyday phenomenon? Can the everyday be heroic? What did you mean by the title?*

2 **A:** Many people think heroism is a quality reserved for an exceptional few, such as Nobel Peace Prize winners or famous leaders.

These are heroes. But these heroes should be idealized and looked to for guidance, like the North Star—a moral compass, not a literal road map[3]. The more I read in researching and creating this book—and learned, and listened—the more obvious it became. The heroes of today are anything but rare. They are everywhere.

Q: *Do you think that we, as a society, do enough to recognize and reward heroism, and thus to encourage it?*

3 **A:** Everyday heroes are standing beside you in the elevator and sitting across from you on the subway; they're your next-door neighbors and your college roommates; they're teachers, doctors, lawyers, inventors, and orphans. There are quiet heroes among us—

[1] **nonprofit:** a business, such as a charity, that does not intend to make money for its owners
[2] **social entrepreneur:** a person who starts businesses to help deal with social problems
[3] **a moral compass, not a literal road map:** an example of an ethical way of living, not a list of rules

ordinary men and women who have devoted themselves to uplifting the lives of others. And it is precisely their ordinariness that makes them extraordinary.

Q: *What do you think we learn from reading the stories of these heroes?*

OUT WITH CHARITY, IN WITH PARTNERSHIP.

4 **A:** Today, there is a shift in the relationship between the giver and the receiver. The handout has been replaced by the handshake. Today's nonprofit reformers are interested in creating meaningful equal partnerships to **empower** communities and individuals to raise themselves out of poverty.

5 Robert Egger founded DC Central Kitchen, which trains people for jobs, distributes meals, and supports local food systems. Doing these things strengthens community and builds long-term solutions to the interconnected problems of poverty, hunger, poor health, and homelessness. Egger said, "A great nonprofit doesn't try to solve the problem; it tries to reveal the power we have as a community to solve the problem."

YOU'RE NEVER TOO YOUNG.

6 The growing group of young social entrepreneurs proves that experience is not necessary for leadership.

7 Rebecca Onie was a sophomore at Harvard when she founded Health Leads, which connects low-income families with the basic resources they need to be healthy.

8 Adam Braun founded Pencils of Promise when he was 25 with a modest $25 deposit. It has raised more than $3 million to build schools in poor developing countries.

YOU'RE NEVER TOO OLD.

9 Roy Prosterman of Landesa, now in his seventies, is the world's leading expert on democratic land reform and a fierce **advocate** for the rights of the rural poor. Through Landesa, formerly known as the Rural Development Institute, he has helped secure land rights for more than 105 million families in 45 developing countries. Prosterman, who continues to work, says, "I'm not tired at all. In fact, it energizes me."

ENTREPRENEURS ARE BORN, NOT MADE.

10 I think that every entrepreneur I interviewed would agree this is true. Most have walked to the beat of their own drum[4] since they took their first uncertain steps as toddlers and have never been satisfied in a conventional professional setting. All believe that risking failure is fundamental. It takes a healthy dose of confidence, courage, and determination to be responsible for others day in and day out.

YOU CAN'T RELY ON THE KINDNESS OF STRANGERS.

11 Because of the growing number of nonprofits, it is harder to get **funding**. Today's social entrepreneurs realize that the surest way to survival is self-sustainability[5].

12 Chuck Slaughter, founder and CEO of Living Goods, has two driving passions: global travel and solving social problems. Living Goods empowers entrepreneurs to deliver life-changing products to the doorsteps of the poor. Slaughter's goal is to make Living Goods a completely self-sustaining business that "fights poverty and disease with profitability."

---

[4] **walk to the beat of their own drum:** to do things the way they want to, not how most people did them
[5] **self-sustainability:** ability to raise enough money to pay for expenses without depending on donations

GO BIG OR GO HOME.

13 Take a small idea and make it huge. The potential for **exponential** growth is practically a necessity for the new social entrepreneurs.

14 Jill Vialet of Playworks, which has helped ensure safe recreational time for 130,000 kids in 300 schools in 23 cities across the U.S., said she spends a lot of time thinking about how Playworks is going to grow enough to change the system. Her ultimate vision is that one day every kid in America will have access to safe, healthy play every day. And she feels it's doable!

TRUE HEROES NEVER CONSIDER THEMSELVES HEROES.

15 If I had a dollar for every time one of these charitable leaders said to me, "You know, the true heroes are the *[blank]*, not me," I'd be $50 richer. They all possess a sense of **humility** and **authenticity** that I've come to realize is essential to the achievement of their visions. The basic fact remains: none of these nonprofits would have succeeded so well without the profound sacrifices of their dedicated founders and CEOs.

16 Eugene Cho, founder and president of One Day's Wages, found the courage to give up one year's wages in the name of service. One Day's Wages has raised more than a million dollars and supports many projects around the world to improve education, deliver clean water, and end poverty.

Q: *How did you find these everyday heroes?*

17 **A:** There were thousands of worthy candidates who deserve to be recognized and celebrated—how to choose just 50? With each hero's story there is yet another example of generosity all around us. There is no contribution too small or insignificant. Whether you choose to show kindness to a loved one or a neighbor, to volunteer, to donate, or to build your own movement—you are helping to grow a culture of giving.

18 Jill Vialet summed it up best, "Believing in the idea that everyone can be an everyday hero is essential to our future as a society. And it's the everyday-ness of it that's more important than the heroism."

B. VOCABULARY Here are some words from Reading 2. Read the word and the three definitions in each row. Two of the definitions are similar and correct. A third is incorrect. Cross out the incorrect definition.

1. **personify** *(v.)*	a. to be a good example of	b. to change someone	c. to represent
2. **humanitarian** *(adj.)*	a. belonging to people	b. caring about people	c. wanting to improve the way people live
3. **diverse** *(adj.)*	a. backward	b. having many differences	c. varied
4. **cause** *(n.)*	a. belief that people fight for	b. organization that people support	c. belief in something that isn't true
5. **perceive** *(v.)*	a. to get from someone	b. to notice	c. to see
6. **phenomenon** *(n.)*	a. someone or something special	b. someone or something difficult	c. someone or something very different or unusual
7. **empower** *(v.)*	a. to calm someone down	b. to encourage someone	c. to give power to someone
8. **advocate** *(n.)*	a. supporter	b. banker	c. promoter
9. **funding** *(n.)*	a. savings in a bank	b. money for a specific purpose	c. financial support for an organization
10. **exponential** *(adj.)*	a. increasing quickly	b. becoming more and more	c. bringing things together
11. **humility** *(n.)*	a. modesty	b. sadness	c. quality of not feeling more important than others
12. **authenticity** *(n.)*	a. quality of being easy to work with	b. quality of being real	c. quality of being what someone seems to be

iQ PRACTICE Go online for more practice with the vocabulary.
Practice › Unit 1 › Activity 7

C. CATEGORIZE Read the statements. Write *T* (true) or *F* (false). Then correct each false statement to make it true according to the interview.

_____ 1. Everyday heroes are ordinary people who help other people.

_____ 2. The social entrepreneurs in the book all have the same goals.

_____ 3. The nonprofits in the book are focused on giving away money.

_____ 4. All nonprofits rely on people to donate money so that the business can continue.

_____ 5. At least one nonprofit leader believes that people need to help themselves.

_____ 6. The heroes in the book seem to be satisfied with helping a small number of people.

D. CATEGORIZE Complete the chart with information about the heroes from the article.

Person	Business	What the business does	Local, national, or international
Roger Egger		trains people for jobs, distributes meals, and supports local food systems	
	Health Leads		
Adam Braun		builds schools in poor developing countries	
	Landesa		international
		fights poverty and disease	international
	Playworks	ensures safe recreational time for kids	
Eugene Cho	One Day's Wages		

E. CATEGORIZE Using the information in the chart on page 16, put the name of each hero in the column (or columns) that describes the focus of his or her company.

Education and training	Health and safety	Legal help
Roger Egger	Roger Egger	

F. EXPLAIN Answer these questions. Discuss your answers with a partner.

1. In paragraph 3, what does the author mean when she says, "… it is precisely their ordinariness that makes them extraordinary"?

2. Using your own words, what is the main idea of paragraph 10?

3. Can someone who doesn't fit the description in paragraph 10 still be a hero? Why or why not?

WORK WITH THE VIDEO

VIDEO VOCABULARY

community (n.) all the people who live in a particular area when talked about as a group

vet (n.) a person who has been trained in the science of animal medicine, whose job is to treat animals who are sick or injured [informal for *veterinarian*]

mate (n.) friend [British and Australian English; informal]

recognize (v.) to admit or to be aware that something exists or is true

A. PREVIEW Do you volunteer in your community? Why? Why not?

iQ RESOURCES Go online to watch the video about a volunteer hairdresser.
Resources > Video > Unit 1 > Unit Video

B. COMPOSE Watch the video two or three times. How do the volunteers help people? Who do they help? Take notes in the first part of the chart.

	Josh Coombes	Jade	Both
Notes from the video			
My ideas			

C. EXTEND What makes Josh and Jade admirable? Write your ideas in the chart above. The video ends by asking if there is something you can give to your community. Can you think of examples of others who could use their skills to help in their community? Discuss your ideas with a partner.

WRITE WHAT YOU THINK

SYNTHESIZE Think about Reading 1, Reading 2, and the unit video as you discuss the questions. Then choose one question and write a paragraph of 5–7 sentences in response.

1. Have you ever volunteered to do something to help your community? If so, describe your experience.

2. Firefighters are often seen as admirable. What other people are seen as admirable because of their profession? Why?

3. Think of someone in the news who is a real-life role model. What makes this person a role model?

VOCABULARY SKILL Using the dictionary

When you look up a word in the dictionary, you will find the definition and other information about the word and how it is used. Different dictionaries may include slightly different information, but they are generally organized in a similar way. Notice the different parts of this dictionary entry from the *Oxford Advanced American Dictionary for learners of English*.

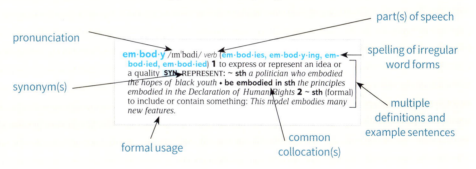

All dictionary entries adapted from the *Oxford Advanced American Dictionary for learners of English* © Oxford University 2011.

A. IDENTIFY Look at the dictionary entry for *mentality*. Check (✓) the information that this entry has.

> **men·tal·i·ty** /mɛnˈtæləţi/ *noun* [usually sing.] (*pl.* **men·tal·i·ties**) the particular attitude or way of thinking of a person or group **SYN** MINDSET: *I cannot understand the mentality of video gamers.* • *a criminal/ghetto mentality*

☐ pronunciation   ☐ example sentence

☐ part(s) of speech   ☐ formal usage

☐ spelling of irregular word forms   ☐ synonym(s)

☐ multiple definitions   ☐ common collocation(s)

TIP FOR SUCCESS
The abbreviations
-sth and -sb mean
"something" and
"somebody." They
show you whether a
verb is followed by a
noun for a thing (-sth),
a person (-sb), or both.

B. IDENTIFY Look at the dictionary entries. Answer the questions. Then compare answers with a partner.

con·front ʔ+ /kənˈfrʌnt/ verb
1 ~ **sb/sth** (of problems or a difficult situation) to appear and need to be dealt with by someone: *the economic problems confronting the country* • *The government found itself confronted by massive opposition.* **2** ~ **sth** to deal with a problem or difficult situation **SYN** FACE UP TO: *She knew that she had to confront her fears.* **3** ~ **sb** to face someone so that they cannot avoid seeing and hearing you, especially in an unfriendly or dangerous situation: *This was the first time he had confronted an armed robber.* **4** ~ **sb with sb/sth** to make someone face or deal with an unpleasant or difficult person or situation: *He confronted her with a choice between her career or their relationship.* **5** **be confronted with sth** to have something in front of you that you have to deal with or react to: *When confronted with a bear, stop and stay calm.*

1. How many definitions does *confront* have? ____

2. What synonym is given for *confront*? _____

3. What common expression is given that uses *confront*?

   _____

in·her·ent ʔ+ Ⓦ /ɪnˈhɪrənt; -ˈhɛr-/ adj. ~ **(in sb/sth)** that is a basic or permanent part of someone or something and that cannot be removed **SYN** INTRINSIC: *the difficulties inherent in a study of this type* • *Violence is inherent in our society.* • *an inherent weakness in the design of the machine* ▸ **in·her·ent·ly** adv.: *an inherently unworkable system*

4. What part of speech is *inherent*? _____

   Inherently? _____

5. What synonym is given for *inherent*? _____

con·strain Ⓦ /kənˈstreɪn/ verb (formal) **1** [usually passive] ~ **sb to do sth** to force someone to do something or behave in a particular way: *The evidence was so compelling that he felt constrained to accept it.* **2** [often passive] to restrict or limit someone or something: ~ **sth** *Research has been constrained by a lack of funds.* • ~ **sb (from doing sth)** *She felt constrained from continuing by the threat of losing her job.*

6. In what form is *constrain* usually used? _____

7. How many example sentences are given for *constrain*? ____

8. What words often follow *constrain*? _____

a·chieve·ment 🔊 **Ⓦ** /əˈtʃiːvmənt/ *noun*
1 [C] a thing that someone has done successfully, especially using their own effort and skill: *the greatest scientific achievement of the decade* ◆ *It was a remarkable achievement for such a young player.* ◆ *They were proud of their children's achievements.* **2** [U] the act or process of achieving something: *the need to raise standards of achievement in education* ◆ *Even a small success gives you a **sense of achievement** (= a feeling of pride).*

9. How many definitions does *achievement* have? ____

10. What common collocation is given that uses *achievement*?

_____

C. EXTEND Work with a partner. Look up words from Readings 1 and 2 in your dictionary. Take turns asking questions like the ones in Activity B.

iQ PRACTICE Go online for more practice with using the dictionary.
Practice ❯ Unit 1 ❯ Activity 8

WRITING

At the end of this unit, you will write an analysis essay about the qualities that make someone admirable. This essay will include specific information from the readings, the unit video, and your own ideas.

WRITING SKILL Organizing and developing an essay

An **analysis essay** examines a topic by breaking it down into smaller parts. Remember that an essay includes an **introduction**, one or more **body paragraphs**, and a **conclusion**.

Introduction

This paragraph should make the reader interested in your topic. It usually includes a "hook" to catch the reader's attention. It also provides background information or general statements about the topic. Within the introduction paragraph, include a **thesis statement**. The thesis statement contains the topic and the **controlling idea** (a specific idea or an opinion about the topic) of the essay. It tells the reader the purpose of the essay.

topic   controlling idea

☐ **Thesis statement:** A role model inspires people to do their best.

Body paragraphs

For each body paragraph, include a **topic sentence** that states the topic of the paragraph and the controlling idea. Add supporting sentences that provide as much detail as possible to fully develop your thesis. Use supporting sentences that all relate to or develop the topic to create **unity**. Organize the supporting sentences in a logical way, so there is a clear connection between the ideas to create **coherence**. Often **transition words** like *first, in addition,* and *for example* are used to show the relationship between supporting ideas.

Conclusion

The conclusion brings the essay to a close. This paragraph may restate the thesis statement in different words, summarize the main points, or do both. Write sentences that remind the reader of why he or she is reading the essay. You can also use the conclusion to help your reader look beyond the essay or think about further ideas that relate to your topic.

iQ RESOURCES Go online to watch the Writing Skill Video.
Resources ❯ Video ❯ Unit 1 ❯ Writing Skill Video

A. WRITING MODEL Read the model essay. Then follow the steps below.

Successful People

1   Are fame and fortune in your future? Do you dream of becoming a billionaire or a famous actor? For most of us, that is not too likely. Even though we may never see our picture on the cover of a glossy magazine, we all want to make something of ourselves and have a good life. We all want to succeed, and identifying what qualities make someone successful can help us to achieve that goal.

2   Successful people share three common qualities that allow them to stand out. First, people who are successful are organized. They don't waste time, and they work in ways that maximize their efficiency. They also work longer hours. Second, they are focused and single-minded. They can see where they want to go, and they only do the things that will get them there. For example, when they are working on something, they don't get lost in the details or overwhelmed by the tasks they need to do. Finally, people who are successful must be able to set and accomplish goals. Knowing what they want helps them stay both organized and focused.

3   If you want to be successful, you need to get organized, stay focused, and set and accomplish goals. Not many people succeed without these qualities, but don't despair. These behaviors can be learned and improved, and anyone can stand out if he or she develops organization, focus, and goals.

1. Read the introduction again. Circle the hook.

2. Find the thesis statement in the introductory paragraph. Underline the topic once. Underline the controlling idea twice.

3. Underline the topic sentence of the body paragraph.

4. One sentence in the body doesn't contribute to the unity of the essay, because it doesn't develop the topic. Draw a line through it.

5. Circle the transition words that contribute to the coherence of the body paragraph.

6. Read the conclusion again. Circle the answer that best describes what the conclusion does.

    a. It restates the thesis statement and suggests further examination of the topic.

    b. It summarizes the main points and suggests ways to be successful.

    c. It restates the thesis statement and summarizes the main points.

B. CREATE In the chart, list two people you consider successful, the qualities you believe contributed to their success, and their accomplishments. List one family member or friend and a famous or well-known person.

Successful people	Qualities	Accomplishments
my mother	hardworking, organized, caring	worked as a nurse while raising my sisters and me

 CRITICAL THINKING STRATEGY

Ordering ideas

To **order your ideas** is to decide which idea should come first, second, third, etc. The order can inform your reader of the relative importance of each point. Transition words can help the reader see not only the order of those points, but also logical connections between the points and explanations or examples you choose to include.

> Successful people share several basic qualities. **First**, they are organized. **Second**, they are focused and single-minded. **For example**, when they are working on something, they don't get lost in the details or overwhelmed by the tasks they need to do. **Finally**, they are goal oriented: they set and accomplish goals.

iQ PRACTICE Go online to watch the Critical Thinking Video and check your comprehension. *Practice ˃ Unit 1 ˃ Activity 9*

C. ANALYZE Work with a partner. Read the sentences and number them to make a logically ordered body paragraph. First, identify the topic sentence. Then order the supporting sentences to create unity and coherence. Then write the whole paragraph in order and check for unity and coherence. Compare your order with a partner and discuss any differences.

____ a. First, role models have a well-developed set of skills or qualities, but they may be unwilling or unable to help others develop them.

____ b. Mentors, on the other hand, may have the same skills or qualities, but they make it a point to train or teach others on a personal basis.

____ c. There are two important differences between role models and mentors.

_3_ d. For example, a research scientist may be great in the lab but not in the classroom.

____ e. Role models may or may not pay personal attention to those they inspire and may affect a large number of people at once, but mentors always have a few special people they work with individually.

____ f. A role model can inspire many people just by his or her actions, while a mentor is limited to inspiring a few people at a time.

____ g. This is because of the time it takes to work with someone individually.

____ h. A second factor is the number of people a role model or mentor can influence at one time.

D. CREATE The paragraph in Activity C is the body paragraph for an essay about role models and mentors. Answer the questions.

1. List some possible hooks for an introduction to this paragraph.

_____

_____

2. Choose the best thesis statement for the essay.

   a. We all need both role models and mentors.

   b. Role models and mentors are both admirable, but their effect on our lives will be very different.

   c. Both role models and mentors are admirable.

3. What is the best way to conclude this essay?

_____

iQ PRACTICE Go online for more practice with organizing and developing an essay. *Practice > Unit 1 > Activity 10*

1. **Restrictive relative clauses*** describe or identify nouns. Usually, they directly follow nouns, noun phrases, or indefinite pronouns (*something, everyone,* etc.).

pronoun /
noun   restrictive relative clause (adjective clause)

A role model is <u>someone</u> **who makes a difference in people's lives.**

Role models face <u>questions</u> **that we may also face.**

2. Most relative clauses begin with a relative pronoun.

   • Use *who* or *that* after nouns for people.

   Role models are <u>people</u> **who may volunteer in their communities.**

   <u>Ordinary people</u> **that we each know** can be role models.

   • Use *that* or *which* after nouns for things. (*Which* usually sounds more formal.)

   <u>Biographies</u> **that tell stories of successful people** are very popular.

   Role models do <u>things</u> **that we would like to do.**

   Sarah works for a <u>company</u> **which helps the homeless.**

3. You can think of a sentence with a relative clause as a combination of two sentences about the same noun.

   • In a **subject relative clause**, the relative pronoun stands for the subject of the clause. It is followed by a verb.

   A role model is someone. + ~~He or she~~ makes a difference in people's lives. =

   subject + verb

   A role model is <u>someone</u> **who makes a difference in people's lives.**

   • In an **object relative clause**, the relative pronoun stands for the object of the clause. The relative pronoun is followed by a subject + verb.

   Role models face questions. + We may also face ~~the questions~~. =

   object + subject + verb

   Role models face <u>questions</u> **that we may also face.**

4. In object relative clauses, the relative pronoun can be omitted.

   <u>Ordinary people</u> ~~that~~ **we each know can be role models.**

   Role models do <u>things</u> ~~that~~ **we would like to do.**

*also called *identifying adjective clauses*

A. IDENTIFY Underline the restrictive relative clause in each sentence. Circle the noun, noun phrase, or indefinite pronoun it identifies.

1. Not every (person) <u>who makes his or her community a better place</u> is acknowledged for it.

2. They do the things that they do because they want to make their communities better.

3. At 19, Ahmed borrowed a book that changed his life forever.

4. His father was an illiterate cattle merchant who insisted that his son have an education.

5. She reads storybooks to children who have no access to television.

6. Maryam started a youth environmental group which is trying to clean up the city.

7. The trash Maryam's group collects is carried away by bicycles.

B. COMPOSE Combine each pair of sentences using a restrictive relative clause with *who*, *that*, or *which*. Use the words in bold to help you.

1. We all aspire to do **something**. Other people will respect **it**.

     We all aspire to do something that other people will respect.

2. Role models may inspire us to help **people**. **They** cannot help themselves.

     _____

3. Role models have **qualities**. We would like to have **them**.

     _____

4. To me, **a person** is a role model. **He** inspires others to do good deeds.

     _____

5. Reading novels gives students **something**. They cannot get **it** in textbooks.

     _____

6. Caring for the environment is **something**. We can all do **it**.

     _____

7. **Someone** is a generous person. **He or she** donates money to charity.

     _____

C. IDENTIFY Which sentences in Activity B can omit the relative pronoun? Cross out the relative pronoun if it can be omitted.

iQ PRACTICE Go online for more practice with restrictive relative clauses.
Practice > Unit 1 > Activities 11–12

Write an analysis essay

In this assignment, you are going to write a three-paragraph analysis essay. As you prepare your essay, think about the Unit Question, "What makes someone admirable?" Use information from Reading 1, Reading 2, the unit video, and your work in this unit to support your essay. Refer to the Self-Assessment checklist on page 30.

iQ PRACTICE Go online to the Writing Tutor to read a model three-paragraph analysis essay. *Practice > Unit 1 > Activity 13*

PLAN AND WRITE

A. BRAINSTORM Follow these steps to help you organize your ideas.

1. In the chart, list three people who you think are admirable. Describe the qualities that they possess and give an example of their accomplishments.

Person	Qualities	Accomplishments
1.		
2.		
3.		

2. Compare the people in your chart. What qualities do they share? How are their accomplishments similar or different?

Similarities	Differences

B. PLAN Follow these steps to plan your essay.

1. Write a topic for your essay.

_____

2. Write an opinion or a specific idea about the topic above. This will be your controlling idea for your thesis statement.

_____

_____

3. Now combine your topic from 1 and your controlling idea from 2 to form your thesis statement.

_____

_____

_____

iQ RESOURCES Go online to download and complete the outline for your analysis essay. *Resources › Writing Tools › Unit 1 › Outline*

C. WRITE Use your planning notes to write your essay.

1. Write your analysis essay about the qualities that make a person admirable. Be sure to have an introduction, a body paragraph, and a conclusion. Include restrictive relative clauses where appropriate. You may also use transition words from the box to help connect your ideas.

In addition,	For example,	First,	Finally,
Also,	For instance,	Second,	Most importantly,

2. Look at the Self-Assessment checklist below to guide your writing.

iQ PRACTICE Go online to the Writing Tutor to write your assignment.
Practice > Unit 1 > Activity 14

REVISE AND EDIT

iQ RESOURCES Go online to download the peer review worksheet.
Resources > Writing Tools > Unit 1 > Peer Review Worksheet

A. **PEER REVIEW** Read your partner's essay. Then use the peer review worksheet. Discuss the review with your partner.

B. **REWRITE** Based on your partner's review, revise and rewrite your essay.

C. **EDIT** Complete the Self-Assessment checklist as you prepare to write the final draft of your essay. Be prepared to hand in your work or discuss it in class.

SELF-ASSESSMENT	Yes	No
Does the essay have an introduction with a hook and thesis statement?	☐	☐
Are there enough details in the body paragraph to support the topic sentence?	☐	☐
If transition words are included, are they used appropriately?	☐	☐
Are restrictive relative clauses used correctly?	☐	☐
Does the essay include vocabulary from the unit?	☐	☐
Did you check the essay for punctuation, spelling, and grammar?	☐	☐

D. **REFLECT** Discuss these questions with a partner or group.

1. What is something new you learned in this unit?

2. Look back at the Unit Question—What makes someone admirable? Is your answer different now than when you started the unit? If yes, how is it different? Why?

iQ PRACTICE Go to the online discussion board to discuss the questions.
Practice > Unit 1 > Activity 15

TRACK YOUR SUCCESS

iQ PRACTICE Go online to check the words and phrases you have learned in this unit. *Practice > Unit 1 > Activity 16*

Check (✓) the skills and strategies you learned. If you need more work on a skill, refer to the page(s) in parentheses.

READING	☐ I can preview and predict the content of a text. (p. 4)
VOCABULARY	☐ I can understand the organization of a dictionary entry. (p. 19)
WRITING	☐ I can organize and develop an essay. (p. 22)
CRITICAL THINKING	☐ I can order ideas to indicate their relative importance. (p. 24)
GRAMMAR	☐ I can use restrictive relative clauses. (p. 26)

OBJECTIVE ▶ ☐ I can gather information and ideas to write an analysis essay about what makes someone admirable.

Behavioral Science

READING highlighting and annotating
CRITICAL THINKING discussing ideas
VOCABULARY collocations with nouns
WRITING writing a descriptive essay
GRAMMAR definite and indefinite articles

How do marketers get our attention?

A. Discuss these questions with your classmates.

1. Where do you get information about products you want to buy?

2. Look at the photo. Is the boy paying attention to the ad? Do you pay attention to ads or ignore them?

B. Listen to *The Q Classroom* online. Then answer these questions.

1. Why are appearances important to Sophy when she makes a purchase? Do you share this value? Why or why not?

2. What does Marcus say about packaging and Felix about presentation? Give other examples of how packaging or presentation affects your decision to buy something.

iQ PRACTICE   Go to the online discussion board to discuss the Unit Question with your classmates. *Practice > Unit 2 > Activity 1*

UNIT OBJECTIVE

Read the articles. Gather information and ideas to write a descriptive essay about an advertisement for a product, business, or service.

Your Guide to Generation Z: The Frugal, Brand-Wary, Determined Anti-Millennials

OBJECTIVE ▶

You are going to read an article by Elizabeth Segran, PhD, a staff writer at the business magazine *Fast Company*. The article discusses what companies need to know about Generation Z. Use the article to gather information and ideas for your Unit Assignment.

PREVIEW THE READING

A. PREVIEW Read the title. Read the caption under the photograph. Answer the questions.

1. Who is Generation Z? What do you think the title means by *anti-millennials*?

2. The Great Recession was a period of economic decline from the end of 2007 through early 2009 and was started by the failure of the housing market. What effect did the Great Recession have on Gen Z?

B. QUICK WRITE How do you decide which product to buy? What influences your decision? Popularity? Quality? Value? Cost? Other factors? What type of information do you look for in advertisements about the product? Write for 5–10 minutes in response. Remember to use this section for your Unit Assignment.

C. VOCABULARY Check (✓) the words you know. Then work with a partner to locate each word in the reading. Use clues to help define the words you don't know. Check your definitions in the dictionary.

allure *(n.)*	**insight** *(n.)* 𝕃+ OPAL
assume *(v.)* 𝕃+ OPAL	**obsession** *(n.)* 𝕃+
disclose *(v.)* 𝕃+	**put a premium on** *(v. phr.)*
distinct *(adj.)* 𝕃+ OPAL	**resistance** *(n.)* 𝕃+ OPAL
endorse *(v.)* 𝕃+	**tolerant** *(adj.)*
exaggerated *(adj.)* 𝕃+	**transparency** *(n.)* 𝕃+

𝕃+ Oxford 5000™ words   OPAL Oxford Phrasal Academic Lexicon

iQ PRACTICE Go online to listen and practice your pronunciation.
Practice ▸ Unit 2 ▸ Activity 2

A. INVESTIGATE Read the article and gather information about Generation Z.

Your Guide to Generation Z:
The Frugal[1], Brand-Wary, Determined Anti-Millennials[2]

by Elizabeth Segran, PhD

The generation forged during the Great Recession

1   For the past several years, the media has been obsessed with millennials, the most studied group ever. But as Generation Z grows up, corporations are paying more attention to these young people, born between 1996 and 2011. At 60 million in the United States, they outnumber millennials by 1 million. It would be easy to **assume** that they are just an **exaggerated** version of the generation that came before them, spending even more of their lives on social media and doing even more shopping online. But Generation Z grew up in a very different historical context than millennials, which has given them a **distinct** outlook on the world.

2   Millennials were Internet pioneers. They invented Facebook, shopped from their smartphones, and smoothly transitioned from satellite TV to Hulu and Netflix. Generation Z, meanwhile, doesn't remember life without these basics of the 21st century. Since many members of Generation Z are just now leaving the nest, it's impossible to draw definitive conclusions about what their habits, lifestyles, and world views will be. But as the oldest start college and careers, we're beginning to see trends emerge.

The Rejection of Big Brands

3   Marketers have been studying Generation Z for many years now, observing their preferences as children and teenagers. They have found that they have a very different relationship with companies than their elders. "Compared to any generation before, they are less trusting of brands," says Emerson Spartz, CEO of the digital media company Dose. "They have the strongest misinformation filter because they've grown up in an era where information was available at all times."

4   For decades, brands communicated through advertisements. Corporations with the biggest budgets could make the biggest impact through billboard, magazine, TV, and radio ads. But with the Internet, people can learn about what brands really stand for, beyond the photoshopped visions they project. Online reviews, for example, have made shoddy[3] products easy to spot. Gen Zers know this better than anyone. They immediately learn when a company has lied to them.

5   Gen Zers are also less conspicuous consumers than their predecessors. There was a time when young people aspired to wear flashy labels conspicuously[4]: Millennials flocked to[5] Hollister and Abercrombie and Fitch. But kids are now showing **resistance** to serving as walking advertisements. As a

[1] **frugal:** using only as much money as necessary
[2] **millennial:** a member of the generation of people who became adults around 2000
[3] **shoddy:** made badly or with not enough care
[4] **conspicuously:** easy to see or notice; likely to attract attention
[5] **flock to:** to go to in large numbers

result, many of the major apparel companies are doing poorly. "They're less brand-conscious and they are not spending as much as millennials do," says Kyle Andrew, chief marketing officer of American Eagle Outfitters. This is a brand that targets teens, which unlike some brands, has seen sales rise.

6   Still, Gen Z is hardly a lost cause for major companies. Spartz says that brands that can communicate with customers in an open way tend to do better with young people. Everlane and Cuyana, for instance, offer **insight** into how products are made. Warby Parker and Tom's make a point of explaining how they try to promote social good. In turn, these companies seem to have attracted the shopping attention of Gen Z. "Authenticity and **transparency** are two ideals that they value highly," he says.

7   Gen Zers also tend to trust individuals more than big corporations. As a result, many brands focused on them are partnering with social media influencers[6] in an effort to appear more relatable. These influencers— their peers—appear on social media, such as Instagram and YouTube, and are paid to **endorse** products. (Influencers are required by law to **disclose** this.) Nevertheless, it works: if a brand is endorsed by someone Gen Z follows, then Gen Z trusts that brand.

Careful Spenders

8   Generation Z doesn't just stand out in the way they relate to brands. They're also spending their money differently. Companies have noticed that young adults **put a premium on** getting good value for their money. Spirit Airlines, for instance, is preparing for Gen Z to become the dominant group of travelers. It is rebranding itself as an ultra-low-cost carrier. The airline offers rock-bottom fares, but with zero frills. Spirit has found that this generation, who are buying their own tickets for the first time, is comfortable paying only for what they are using. Rana Ghosh, an executive at Spirit says. "It's not so much that they are price-conscious; it's about what they are getting for the money they spend."

9   Gen Z also tends to be savvy in their approach to electronics, resisting the **allure** of the latest, priciest products when there is a constant stream of new, inexpensive options. "Technological innovation is no longer an exciting, celebrated thing as much as an expectation," says Sam Paschel, chief commercial officer of the headphone brand Skullcandy. The brand targets younger consumers. "Generation Z relates to technology as a tool, as opposed to an **obsession**," Paschel says. To keep up with the demands of today's teens, the company has invested heavily in scientists and researchers who work to improve the quality of sound. At the same time, Skullcandy has avoided flashy advertising or even charging a premium for its product. Rather, it strives for subtler messaging that speaks to young consumers.

Ultra-Competitive, But Very Accepting

10   Market research also suggests that while Generation Z is an independent generation, they are also inclusive and **tolerant** of difference. With this knowledge, American Eagle Outfitters has tried to incorporate these ideals into its marketing, including an e-commerce website and ad campaigns that are diverse. Ads feature models from a wide range of ethnicities, with a variety of hair textures and body types. Company CMO Andrew says because teens no longer rely on mass-market brands to help them express their identity, AEO is trying to sell teens on creating their own personal brand.

11   Daunted or not, marketers are trying to keep up with the demands of Generation Z. "The rate of change in society is increasing exponentially," Dose CEO Spartz says. "The world is changing more in ten years now than it used to change in 100 years."

---

[6] **influencer:** a person who has the power to affect the purchase decisions of others because of his or her real/perceived authority, knowledge, or position

B. VOCABULARY Here are some words and phrases from Reading 1. Read the sentences. Circle the answer that best matches the meaning of each bold word.

1. He **assumed** that they would buy the product because others had bought it.

   a. thought   b. proved

ACADEMIC LANGUAGE
The corpus shows that *greater than* is often used in academic writing.

_____ OPAL
Oxford Phrasal Academic Lexicon

2. The **exaggerated** number made the ad's effectiveness seem greater than it really was.

   a. accurate   b. overstated

3. Her **distinct** appearance meant that people noticed her.

   a. plain   b. different

4. Because of **resistance** to the plan, he changed it.

   a. agreement   b. opposition

5. By sharing our experience, we hoped to provide the company **insight** about the problem.

   a. understanding   b. answers

6. We need the process to have **transparency** by being open to the public.

   a. clarity   b. secrecy

7. I hope they will **endorse** the product.

   a. say they want   b. say they like

8. The company should **disclose** information, so consumers know the risks.

   a. reveal   b. hide

9. Like most consumers, they **put a premium on** a good deal.

   a. value and want   b. accept and pay for

10. The **allure** of the city, including the nightlife, convinced her to accept the job.

    a. attraction   b. size

11. His has an **obsession** with video games. He plays them constantly.

    a. preoccupation   b. fascination

12. They are **tolerant** of his ideas, but they seldom use them.

    a. able to believe   b. able to accept

iQ PRACTICE Go online for more practice with vocabulary.
Practice > Unit 2 > Activity 3

C. EXPLAIN Answer the questions.

1. What is the main idea of the article?

   _____

2. Who is the audience?

   _____

3. Why are there references to different companies?

   _____

4. What does Emerson Spartz, CEO of the digital media company Dose, mean by "Authenticity and transparency are two ideals that they value highly"?

   _____

5. Where does Gen Z find peers who are influencers? What do they trust them to do?

   _____

D. CATEGORIZE Read the statements. Check (✓) the statements that are true of Generation Z. Correct each false statement to make it true according to the article. Write the paragraph number where the answer is found.

Generation Z

☐ 1. outnumbers millennials. (paragraph ___)

☐ 2. is a younger version of the millennials. (paragraph ___)

☐ 3. grew up in a context similar to that of millennials. (paragraph ___)

☐ 4. is a group of Internet pioneers. (paragraph ___)

☐ 5. doesn't remember a time without technology. (paragraph ___)

☐ 6. has a different relationship with companies than millennials. (paragraph ___)

☐ 7. is trusting of brands. (paragraph ___)

☐ 8. spends more money than millennials. (paragraph ___)

☐ 9. trusts its peers more than companies. (paragraph ___)

☐ 10. is tolerant of difference. (paragraph ___)

E. IDENTIFY Match the companies to information from the reading.

___ 1. American Eagle Outfitters   a. promotes social good.

___ 2. Everlane   b. creates ads that are diverse.

___ 3. Tom's   c. knows Gen Z wants value for its money.

___ 4. Spirit Airlines   d. offers insight into how products are made.

___ 5. Skullcandy   e. invests in science and improving quality.

F. CATEGORIZE Complete the chart with information about Generation Z and millennials.

Generation Z	Millennials
Born between 1996 and 2011	

G. SYNTHESIZE Look back at your Quick Write on page 34. How do you decide which product to buy? Add any new ideas or information you learned from the reading.

iQ PRACTICE Go online for additional reading and comprehension.
Practice > Unit 2 > Activity 4

WRITE WHAT YOU THINK

A. DISCUSS Discuss the questions in a group. Think about the Unit Question, "How do marketers get our attention?"

1. What are some brands that you trust? Why do you trust them?

2. What makes a company trustworthy? How do you get reliable information about companies and products?

3. If you were asked for advice on how marketers should get your attention, what advice would you give?

B. SYNTHESIZE Choose one of the questions from Activity A and write a paragraph of 5–7 sentences in response. Look back at your Quick Write on page 34 as you think about what you learned.

READING SKILL Highlighting and annotating

The purpose of **highlighting** and **annotating** is to identify important ideas in a text. Both of these techniques will allow you to quickly find the information later, without having to reread the text.

Highlighting

Always decide the purpose of your highlighting before you begin. Then highlight, underline, or circle information in a text such as:

- the main idea or topic of a paragraph
- keywords, details, or examples
- phrases that summarize the information

Use different-colored highlighter pens for different types of information. For example, use one color for main ideas and another for details. Or use a graphic system, such as solid lines, dotted lines, circling, etc.

Annotating

Annotating—writing notes directly on the page of a text—is a useful way to identify and mark important information. First, read a paragraph and decide what is important. Then write brief notes in the margin. You may use abbreviations such as these:

T = thesis	S = summary	R = reason
MI = main idea	Ex = example	? = question

A. IDENTIFY Read this paragraph from Reading 1 and look at the highlighting and annotations. Then answer the questions.

Marketers have been studying Generation Z for many years now, observing their preferences as children and teenagers. They have found that they have a very different relationship with companies than their elders. "Compared to any generation before, they are less trusting of brands," says Emerson Spartz, CEO of the digital media company Dose. "They have the strongest misinformation filter ? because they've grown up in an era where information was available at all times."

grew up when information available at all times

1. What does the information highlighted in yellow show? _____

2. What does the information highlighted in pink show? _____

3. What is the purpose of each annotation?

_____

_____

TIP FOR SUCCESS

After annotating the text, you may want to write out your notes to use as a reference and study tool.

B. IDENTIFY Highlight and annotate the following paragraph, taken from Reading 1. Follow these steps. Then compare notes with a partner.

1. Highlight in one color (or circle) the main idea of the paragraph.

2. Highlight in another color (or underline) the key details.

3. Underline an example and write a note in the margin that identifies the specific example.

4. Write a brief note in the margin to summarize the paragraph.

> For decades, brands communicated through advertisements. Corporations with the biggest budgets could make the biggest impact through billboard, magazine, TV, and radio ads. But with the Internet, people can learn about what brands really stand for, beyond the photoshopped visions they project. Online reviews, for example, have made shoddy products easy to spot. Gen Zers know this better than anyone. They immediately learn when a company has lied to them.

iQ PRACTICE Go online for more practice with highlighting and annotating.
Practice ⟩ Unit 2 ⟩ Activity 5

This Is Why You're Addicted to Your Phone

You are going to read an article by Nick Arnold for the BBC news service. The article looks at how technology influences our behavior. Use the article to gather information and ideas for your Unit Assignment.

PREVIEW THE READING

A. PREVIEW The article contains a number references to technology and the Internet. Skim the article to find the answers to these questions.

1. What websites and apps are mentioned in the article?

2. Why do you think these names are mentioned?

B. QUICK WRITE Think about your activities over the past day or so. What media sources have been vying for your attention (notifications on your phone, TV commercials, marketing emails, etc.)? How have you responded? Write for 5–10 minutes in response. Be sure to use this section for your Unit Assignment.

C. VOCABULARY Check (✓) the words you know. Use a dictionary to define any new or unknown words. Then discuss with a partner how the words will relate to the unit.

activation *(n.)* 𝕃+	essentially *(adv.)* 𝕃+ OPAL
align *(v.)* 𝕃+	functional *(adj.)* 𝕃+ OPAL
broadly speaking *(adv. phr.)*	impulsive *(adj.)*
counter *(v.)* 𝕃+	manipulate *(v.)* 𝕃+
crave *(v.)*	metric *(n.)*
escalate *(v.)* 𝕃+	tactic *(n.)* 𝕃+

𝕃+ Oxford 5000™ words   OPAL Oxford Phrasal Academic Lexicon

iQ PRACTICE Go online to listen and practice your pronunciation.
Practice › Unit 2 › Activity 6

WORK WITH THE READING

 A. INVESTIGATE Read the article and gather information about how much technology influences our behavior.

THIS IS WHY YOU'RE ADDICTED TO YOUR PHONE

BY NICK ARNOLD

1   In 2015, Max Stossel, 28, had an awakening. He was a successful social media strategist[1] working with major multinational companies. But that same year, he realized that some of the work he was doing wasn't actually in people's best interests. Stossel has since become a pivotal part of the Time Well Spent movement. It "aims to **align** technology with our human values."

2   Time Well Spent was co-founded by the former Google "product philosopher" Tristan Harris. It is made up of "a group of industry insiders," many of whom have worked for companies like Facebook and Snapchat but have now aligned themselves with the movement in some way. Last year, Ofcom, the UK communications regulator, found that more than half of all Internet users in Britain feel they're addicted to technology. "There's this idea that we're addicted to our phones, and that we've done this to ourselves," says Stossel. "That is just not true."

3   Stossel explains that tech design is increasingly informed by behavioral psychology and neuroscience. Tristan Harris himself studied at Stanford's Persuasive Tech Lab, which describes itself as creating "insight into how computing products can be designed to influence and change human behavior." The Lab's website states, "Technology is being designed to change what we think and do." It gives several examples of this from Facebook, YouTube, and Twitter.

4   "When you understand neuroscience and you understand how to develop apps, you can **essentially** program the brain," Stossel says. "There are thousands of people on the other side of your screens whose job it is to keep you as hooked as possible, and they've gotten very good at it."

5   I ask Stossel just how good these people are. I control my notifications, not vice versa, I tell him. He asks a simple question: "Do you feel at all stressed when your phone is out of reach and it buzzes?" Um. Yes. Figuring out how to capture my attention like that, is, according to Stossel, "the job of everybody in my industry."

6   **Broadly speaking**, tech design seeks to take advantage of our brain's reward system, where dopamine[2] **activation** leads to feelings of satisfaction and pleasure. Our brains are programmed to seek more of whatever gives us this pleasure—so much so that we **crave** it when we don't have it. The same system that

[1] **social media strategist:** a person who helps websites or apps succeed   [2] **dopamine:** a chemical produced by nerve cells

makes us crave drugs or certain foods can also make us crave particular apps, games, sites, and devices.

7   But Time Well Spent believes this problem isn't exclusively a tech one. Stossel points out how the ways that content is created—including negative headlines and clickbait[3] **tactics**—can also fit into this type of persuasion. "The problem is that it's everything," he says. "It's all of the life that we live in. Life has become an "attention economy," Stossel explains. "Everybody wants to grab as much of our attention as possible. I was designing notification structures to help take you out of your world and bring you into mine."

8   Stossel argues that users are not the customers of technology, but the products. Our attention is the thing being sold. "We use lots of platforms for free," he says. But advertisers pay the platforms money to get our attention while we're on there. "We're not the ones paying, so the things that matter to us go second to what matters to advertisers," says Stossel.

9   Success in the tech world is often measured using the **metric** of "time spent"—that is, how long we spend using an app, streaming a service, or browsing a website. An example is the way videos auto-play on certain platforms. This keeps more people online for longer. But, Stossel says, "that doesn't mean that they actually want to stay online for longer." Stossel believes that this constant demand for our attention is making us lose focus on the things that are really important.

10   In the days following my conversation with Stossel, I notice how often I get sucked into aimlessly moving through the Instagram stories of people I don't even know. What starts as a mindless scroll through my Facebook feed before bed can easily **escalate** into huge periods of wasted time. I can certainly see the merit of what Time Well Spent is campaigning for. But the sheer scale of change needed leaves me wondering if their fight might be impossibly idealistic.

11   "It is absolutely possible," Stossel **counters**. "The challenge is getting consumers to demand it." He believes technology will **manipulate** our attention in ever more effective ways. "The future will be so good at this. That's why we need to demand this change now." Until that change comes, Time Well Spent co-founder Harris adheres to certain lifestyle changes the movement has designed for living better in the attention economy:

- He's turned off almost all notifications on his phone and has customized the vibration for text messages. Now he can feel the difference between an automated alert and a human's.

- He's made the first screen of his phone almost empty, with only **functional** apps like Uber and Google Maps. He can't get sucked into spending hours on these.

- He's put any apps he's inclined to waste time on, or any apps with colorful, attention-grabbing icons, inside folders on the second page of his phone. To open an app, he types its name into the phone's search bar—which reduces **impulsive** clicks.

- He also has a sticky note on his laptop. What does it say? "Do not open without intention."

---

[3] **clickbait:** material put on the Internet in order to attract attention and encourage visitors to click on a link to a particular web page

B. VOCABULARY Complete each sentence with the vocabulary from Reading 2. You may need to change the form of some of the words.

activation *(n.)*	crave *(v.)*	impulsive *(adj.)*
align *(v.)*	escalate *(v.)*	manipulate *(v.)*
broadly speaking *(adv. phr.)*	essentially *(adv.)*	metric *(n.)*
counter *(v.)*	functional *(adj.)*	tactic *(n.)*

1. When I heard her argument, I wasn't sure how to _____ it with a better one.

2. The _____ we used to measure success in our business was whether we made any money.

3. That desk doesn't _____ with the others in that row; its position is wrong.

4. The business methods that my company uses are based on ethical practices; they are moral _____.

5. Smartphones aren't purely _____: they are also fashion items and people care about what they look like as well as what they can do.

6. _____, web designers want to keep you looking at their websites.

7. My sudden decision to buy these clothes was _____.

8. Playing computer games can quickly _____ from fun to a serious problem.

9. In a sentence, the job of advertisers is _____ to persuade us to buy a product or service.

10. A successful website can _____ us into staying online even if we don't want to.

11. When I get up in the morning, I _____ a cup of hot coffee; I really want one.

12. I could use that website as soon as I signed up: _____ was immediate.

iQ PRACTICE Go online for more practice with the vocabulary.
Practice > Unit 2 > Activity 7

C. INTERPRET Choose an answer. Then explain your answer to a partner.

1. What is the main idea of the article?

   a. We are addicted to our phones, and we have done this to ourselves.

   b. We are addicted to our phones, but tech professionals are trained to addict us.

   c. We are not really addicted to our phones; that idea comes from advertisers.

2. Who is the audience for this article?

   a. website designers

   b. anyone who accesses the Internet

   c. only teenagers

3. What is the purpose of the article?

   a. to inform readers about how they are being manipulated

   b. to tell website and app designers how to make better apps

   c. to encourage readers to stay online

4. What is the purpose of paragraph 3?

   a. to support the idea that we are responsible for our addictions to our phones

   b. to support the idea that advertisers pay for us to stay online

   c. to support the idea that technology is designed to be addictive

5. What is the purpose of paragraph 5?

   a. to demonstrate to tech workers that their tactics work

   b. to demonstrate to the author that he is addicted to his phone

   c. to demonstrate to Stossel that his argument is correct

D. EXPLAIN Answer these questions about the article.

1. According to the article, the Time Well Spent movement "aims to align technology with our human values." What might one of those values be?

   _____

2. Many of the people working with Time Well Spent used to work at social media and tech companies. Why do you think they no longer work for these companies?

   _____

3. When Stossel says, "There are thousands of people on the other side of your screens whose job it is to keep you as hooked as possible," what does he mean?

   _____

4. What is the "attention economy"? Why is it a problem?

   _____

E. RESTATE The article describes changes that Tristan Harris has made. Fill in the chart with information from the article.

What he did	Reason
1. He has turned off almost all notifications . . .	*so his phone doesn't bother him*
2. He set two different vibrations for text messages . . .	
3.	so he can get to "functional" apps but can't see more attractive apps
4. He put attractive icons inside folders on his phone . . .	
5.	to remind him to open apps intentionally

F. DISCUSS Why has Harris done these things? Discuss with a partner.

 CRITICAL THINKING STRATEGY

Discussing ideas

Many questions require you to discuss your ideas. **Discussion** is the exchange of ideas and opinions about a topic. In Activity F, you shared your ideas about Tristan Harris. Listening to your partner's ideas may have provided other ideas. Through discussion, you can clarify your understanding of new material, which will help you remember it better. Listening to others can provide different perspectives.

iQ PRACTICE Go online to watch the Critical Thinking Skill Video and check your comprehension. *Practice > Unit 2 > Activity 8*

G. APPLY Read the ideas for having a good discussion. Check (✓) the ideas that you agree with and make notes about why. Give an example of each point using ideas from this unit. Then discuss your answers with a partner.

☐ 1. prepare what to say ahead of time

☐ 2. refer back to the text to support your ideas

☐ 3. actively follow what others are saying

☐ 4. wait for someone to invite you to speak

☐ 5. take notes on what others say

☐ 6. ask information questions

☐ 7. make the discussion a competition

☐ 8. ask for clarification

☐ 9. restate information to make it clearer

WORK WITH THE VIDEO

A. PREVIEW Do you want companies to gather data about you for marketing purposes? Why? Why not?

VIDEO VOCABULARY

data mining (n.) looking at large amounts of information that has been collected on a computer and using it to provide new information

data set (n.) a collection of data which is treated as a single unit by a computer

instantaneously (adv.) immediately

simultaneously (adv.) at the same time as something else

iQ RESOURCES Go online to watch the video about predictive advertising.
Resources › Video › Unit 2 › Unit Video

B. COMPOSE Watch the video two or three times. Take notes in the chart.

	Data mining	How used in advertising
Notes from the video		

C. EXTEND What are some advantages and disadvantages of personalized advertising? Discuss your ideas with a partner.

WRITE WHAT YOU THINK

SYNTHESIZE Think about Reading 1, Reading 2, and the unit video as you discuss these questions. Then choose one question and write a paragraph of 5–7 sentences in response.

1. Do you trust a company more when it gives you a lot of product information? Why? Why not?

2. What makes you look at an online advertisement?

3. Marketers use sound (e.g., notifications and auto-play ads) and visuals (e.g., color or motion) to grab our attention. Which do you think affects you more?

VOCABULARY SKILL Collocations with nouns

Collocations are words that often occur together. While there are no rules to help you learn collocations, it is important to pay attention to the patterns of words in a text. These patterns are clues that show you which words collocate. There are several common collocation patterns with nouns.

Adjective + noun

- Millennials spend much of their lives on **social media**.
- Tech design seeks to take advantage of our brain's **reward system**.

Verb + noun/noun phrase

- Corporations **are paying more attention to** these young people.
- We **lose focus** on the things that are really important.

Preposition + noun/noun phrase

- **As a result,** many brands are partnering with social media influencers.
- Some of the work he was doing wasn't actually **in people's best interests**.

TIP FOR SUCCESS
Some collocations are idioms. This means that when the words are combined, they take on a unique meaning. Some examples of idioms are *put a premium on* and *pay attention to*.

A. APPLY Circle the word that usually goes together with the bold noun in each sentence. Look back at Reading 1 (R1) and Reading 2 (R2) to check your answers.

1. It's impossible to *get / draw* definitive **conclusions** about what their habits, lifestyles, and world views will be. (R1, paragraph 2)

2. *Online / E-based* **reviews** . . . have made shoddy products easy to spot. (R1, paragraph 4)

3. *By / In* **turn**, these companies seem to have attracted the shopping attention of Gen Z. (R1, paragraph 6)

4. The company **has invested** heavily *in / on* scientists and researchers who work to improve the quality of sound. (R1, paragraph 9)

5. The headphone brand Skullcandy. . . *targets / marks* younger **consumers**. (R1, paragraph 11)

6. **The rate** *for / of* **change** in society is increasing exponentially. (R1, paragraph 11)

7. He was . . . working with major *multination / multinational* **companies**. (R2, paragraph 1)

8. [They] have now aligned themselves with the movement *at / in* **some way**. (R2, paragraph 2)

9. Products can be designed to influence and change *human / person* **behavior**. (R2, paragraph 3)

10. There are thousands of people *in / on* **the other side** of your screens. (R2, paragraph 4)

11. Figuring out how to *capture / imprison* **my attention** . . . is . . . "the job of everybody in my industry." (R2, paragraph 5)

12. Tristan Harris adheres to certain *lifestyle / way of life* **changes**. (R2, paragraph 11)

B. **CREATE** Look at these collocations from Readings 1 and 2. Write sentences using six of the collocations.

Reading 1:	Reading 2:
offer insight into	a person's best interest
social media influencers	grab our attention
show resistance to	use an app
personal brand	stream a service
see trends emerge	browse a website
price-conscious	scroll through a Facebook feed
social good	turn off notifications
good value	

iQ PRACTICE Go online for more practice with collocations with nouns. *Practice > Unit 2 > Activity 9*

WRITING

OBJECTIVE ▶

At the end of this unit, you will write a descriptive essay about an advertisement for a product, business, or service. This essay will include specific information from the readings, the unit video, and your own ideas.

WRITING SKILL Writing a descriptive essay

A **descriptive essay** describes a person, place, or thing in a way that gives the reader a clear mental picture of the subject of the essay.

Organization

- The **introduction** should make the reader interested in what you are describing. It should include a **thesis statement** that tells why the person, place, or thing is your focus.
- Write one or more **body paragraphs** that contain the details of your description.
- Finish with a **conclusion** that gives your final thoughts or opinion about what you are describing.

Descriptive language

A good descriptive essay gives a clear mental picture of the subject of the essay. The reader should be able to imagine that he or she is with the person described, at the place described, etc. Include strong **imagery** (language that helps create these mental pictures) in your body paragraphs.

Not descriptive

She walked into the room.

He was dressed formally.

The street was filled with people selling food.

Descriptive

She walked **slowly** and **nervously** into the **dark** room.
(with adjectives and adverbs)

He wore **a light suit, a silk tie, and shiny shoes**.
(with details and specific language)

The street was filled with **loud men shouting out orders above the smoky smell of grilling meat**.
(with sensory language related to sounds, smells, etc.)

A. WRITING MODEL Read the model descriptive essay. Then follow the steps below.

My Favorite Restaurant

1   One of my favorite restaurants is Ben's Diner on Fourth Street because it's perfect for a casual, delicious meal. Ben's is a family business that has been serving the local community for over 60 years. Look for the red neon sign with its flashing knife and fork. When you see it, you know you can expect good food that was cooked with fresh, local ingredients.

2   As soon as you step through the door at Ben's, you'll be glad you came. The restaurant is brightly lit and spotlessly clean, with gleaming tables and sparkling floors. You'll get a warm welcome from one of the staff, who will take you to a comfortable seat. I like the soft red leather seats in the booths, or sometimes I sit at the smooth marble counter. The pleasant noise of conversation and the soothing clatter of dishes will surround you. If you're not already hungry, the rich smell of homemade chicken soup coming from the kitchen will get you ready to eat.

3   Ben's menu has some old favorites and some unexpected surprises. The perfectly grilled burger is made of 100 percent prime beef. Served on a soft toasted bun, it's crunchy on the outside and moist and peppery inside. Add some sharp cheddar cheese for a satisfying treat. The Greek salad is famous for its fresh ingredients: bright green lettuce leaves, deep red tomatoes, and tangy purple olives. Or how about chicken fajitas, served beside your table in a sizzling skillet, with a spicy aroma I can't resist?

4   So, whether you're looking for somewhere new to get some great food or just passing through, I suggest you head over to Ben's. You'll feel right at home and enjoy some good cooking, too.

1. Underline the thesis statement and the concluding sentence.

2. Find at least two sensory details for each sense.

    a. sight: _red neon sign,_ _____

    b. sound: _____

    c. taste: _____

    d. smell: _____

    e. touch: _____

B. RESTATE Read the sentences. Rewrite them to make them more descriptive. Add adjectives and adverbs, details and specific language, and sensory language. Be creative.

1. The man lived in a house far from the city.

    The old man lived quietly in a small farmhouse far from the busy city.

2. The room was filled with roses, daisies, and lilacs.

    _____

    _____

3. The chicken and potatoes were good.

    _____

    _____

4. We went on a hike though the forest.

    _____

    _____

5. His aunt entered the room.

    _____

    _____

6. I didn't get to watch the soccer game on TV.

    _____

    _____

C. WRITING MODEL Read the model descriptive essay. Then answer the questions that follow.

Adventure Seekers Wanted

1   Do you live for your next escape from your everyday routine? Are you a strong and healthy outdoor person seeking your next great adventure? The Adventurer sport utility vehicle (SUV) is the right vehicle to buy for adventure and outdoor fun if you are a thrill-seeking, athletic person who spends time outdoors. The Adventurer is the best, most reliable SUV to take you, your thrill-seeking friends, and all your gear where you're going, and it will get you there in great comfort and style.

2   Do you spend time climbing snow-capped mountains, rafting through red rock canyons on a raging river, or cruising the rocky shoreline of a vast ocean seeking the perfect wave? If you answered yes to any of these questions, then you know that you need to be driving a powerful, all-wheel-drive vehicle to arrive at your destination. The new Adventurer delivers that power and maneuverability. Don't be fooled by the quiet, comfortable ride. The new Adventurer is the perfect off-road vehicle. It is a powerful, all-wheel-drive vehicle that is as at home on steep, rough dirt roads as it is on a flat, smooth highway. And, as a hybrid, it is the environmentally friendly vehicle you want to drive.

3   Do you plan to take friends and need to carry a lot of gear to your next adventure? There is plenty of room for all the equipment you'll need. The interior of the Adventurer is roomy and comfortable, so you can bring along as many as five fun-loving friends. The seats, of the softest, finest-quality leather, will keep you cool in the heat of the summer and warm in the winter. The climate control air system keeps the interior at a steady, regulated temperature.

4   Each adventure seeker creates his or her own story. Whatever your story, the Adventurer is the means to get you there. You will want the Adventurer because it is the right choice for your healthy, active lifestyle. Test-drive yours today!

1. What is the product?

_____

2. What is the controlling idea about the product?

_____

3. Who is the target customer for the product?

_____

4. What makes the product appealing?

_____

_____

_____

5. What does the conclusion do?

_____

6. Can you form a mental picture of the Adventurer SUV? Explain your answer.

_____

_____

_____

D. CATEGORIZE Look at the graphic organizer, a cluster diagram the author used to organize the description of the Adventurer. Complete the cluster diagram with ideas from the essay and your own ideas.

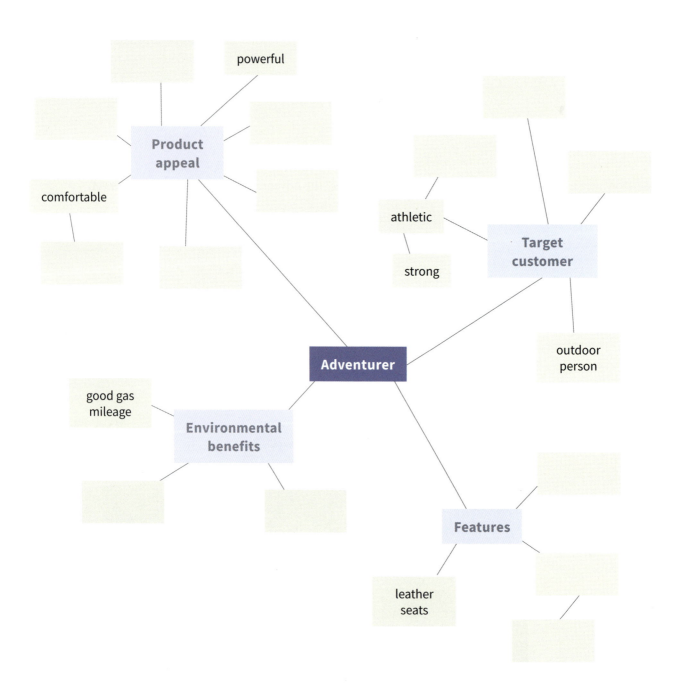

iQ PRACTICE Go online for more practice writing a descriptive essay.
Practice > Unit 2 > Activity 10

A noun (a person, place, thing, or idea) is often introduced by an **article**. Different types of nouns can use different articles. Understanding the context in which a noun occurs will help you use articles correctly.

Singular count noun	Plural count noun	Noncount noun
Indefinite article: *a* + consonant sound *an* + vowel sound	No article	No article
Definite article: *the*	Definite article: *the*	Definite article: *the*

Indefinite article, no article

Use the indefinite article *a/an* when a noun is not specifically identified or is unknown to the reader, for example, on first mention of the noun.

☐ We were excited to have **a new car**.

   (This is the first reference to *a new car*. The reader does not know about it yet.)

Use no article with plural count nouns and noncount nouns to refer to something in general.

☐ **Marketers** have been studying Generation Z for a long time.

   (*Marketers* refers to any marketers, not specific marketers.)

☐ We bought **fish** for dinner.

   (No article is used with noncount nouns.)

Definite articles

Use *the* when a noun is specifically identified. Both the reader and the writer know the noun because they share information about it. For example:

☐ We were excited to have a new car, but **the car** we chose was terrible!

   (*A new car* was introduced earlier in the sentence.)

☐ Let's go to Ben's Diner. **The owners** are really friendly, and **the soup** is delicious.

   (The reader and writer both know that *the owners* refers to the owners of Ben's Diner, and *the soup* is served at Ben's Diner.)

☐ With **the Internet**, people can learn about what brands really stand for.

   (There is only one Internet. It is unique.)

☐ **The government** should do more about false advertising.

   (You can assume the reader will know which government you are referring to.)

iQ RESOURCES Go online to watch the Grammar Skill Video.
Resources > Video > Unit 2 > Grammar Skill Video

TIP FOR SUCCESS

Using *the* is not the only way to refer to
a specific noun.
You may also identify specific nouns with possessive adjectives (*my, your, their,* etc.), demonstrative adjectives (*this*, *that*, *these*, and *those*), or quantifiers (*two*, *many*, *some*, etc.).

APPLY Complete the blog. Write the correct articles: *a/an, the,* or Ø for no article.

| Home | | 🔍 | Sign in 👤 |

So you want to be _____ social media
                              1
influencer? _____ job isn't as easy as you
                2
might imagine. First, you have to be likable. You

need to seem like _____ person who would
                          3
be _____ good friend, and like _____
        4   5
good friend, you should share _____
                                          6
information freely without thinking about

_____ money you might be making from advertising.
      7

   You also have to be interesting. The longer you keep _____
                                                                      8
attention of your followers, the more likely you are to influence them.

Show _____ curiosity about _____ world around you, and make it
          9   10
fun to follow you.

   If you have _____ corporate sponsor, make sure that you and
                      11

_____ company you represent are compatible. You need to look and
      12
sound authentic because today's consumers are savvy about _____
                                                                          13
social media. Show _____ passion that you have for _____ issue
                          14   15
or product you talk about. Speak with _____ honesty, and show
                                                  16

_____ people _____ true reasons for your opinions.
      17   18

   Follow these guidelines, and you will be on _____ way to
                                                            19
becoming _____ influencer.
                20

iQ PRACTICE Go online for more practice with definite and indefinite articles, and no articles with generic nouns. *Practice > Unit 2 > Activities 11–12*

Write a descriptive essay

In this assignment, you are going to write a four-paragraph essay describing an advertisement for a product, business, or service. As you prepare your essay, think about the Unit Question, "How do marketers get our attention?" Use information from Reading 1, Reading 2, the unit video, and your work in this unit to support your essay. Refer to the Self-Assessment checklist on page 60.

iQ PRACTICE Go online to the Writing Tutor to read a model descriptive essay. *Practice > Unit 2 > Activity 13*

PLAN AND WRITE

A. BRAINSTORM Follow these steps to help you organize your ideas.

1. Think of some products, businesses, and services that you trust. These could be things like companies, brands, restaurants, stores, or products like new technology.

2. Browse the Internet or look through magazines for advertisements for these products, businesses, and services.

   a. What features of the advertisements attract your attention? Is there sound? Is there color? Is there movement?

   b. What do you dislike about the advertisement?

   c. How would you describe the advertisements? Think about descriptive language you can use.

3. Choose one product, business, or service advertisement that interests you.

WRITING TIP
You can use a **cluster diagram** to help you organize and develop your ideas. See page 56 for an example.

B. PLAN Follow these steps to plan your essay.

1. Choose two or three main features or qualities of the ads you found in step 2 of Activity A.

2. Brainstorm some descriptive language to give a clear mental picture of each feature or quality you selected.

iQ RESOURCES   Go online to download and complete the outline for your descriptive essay. *Resources > Writing Tools > Unit 2 > Outline*

C. WRITE Use your planning notes to write your essay.

1. Write your essay describing an advertisement for a product, business, or service. Be sure to include a thesis statement that tells why it is your focus and body paragraphs that describe the specific features or qualities of the advertisement.

2. Look at the Self-Assessment checklist on page 60 to guide your writing.

iQ PRACTICE   Go online to the Writing Tutor to write your assignment. *Practice > Unit 2 > Activity 14*

REVISE AND EDIT

iQ RESOURCES Go online to download the peer review worksheet.
Resources > Writing Tools > Unit 2 > Peer Review Worksheet

A. PEER REVIEW Read your partner's essay. Then use the peer review worksheet. Discuss the review with your partner.

B. REWRITE Based on your partner's review, revise and rewrite your essay.

C. EDIT Complete the Self-Assessment checklist as you prepare to write the final draft of your essay. Be prepared to hand in your work or discuss it in class.

SELF-ASSESSMENT	Yes	No
Does the thesis statement have a topic and controlling idea?	☐	☐
Does the essay use descriptive language to create a clear mental picture of the subject?	☐	☐
Are correct articles used?	☐	☐
Did you use collocations from the unit correctly?	☐	☐
Does your essay include vocabulary from the unit?	☐	☐
Did you check the essay for correct punctuation, spelling, and grammar?	☐	☐

D. REFLECT Discuss these questions with a partner or group.

1. What is something new you learned in this unit?

2. Look back at the Unit Question—How do marketers get our attention? Is your answer different now than when you started the unit? If yes, how is it different? Why?

iQ PRACTICE Go to the online discussion board to discuss the questions.
Practice > Unit 2 > Activity 15

TRACK YOUR SUCCESS

iQ PRACTICE   Go online to check the words and phrases you have learned in this unit. *Practice > Unit 2 > Activity 16*

Check (✓) the skills and strategies you learned. If you need more work on a skill, refer to the page(s) in parentheses.

READING ☐ I can highlight and annotate a text. (p. 40)

CRITICAL THINKING ☐ I can discuss ideas. (p. 47)

VOCABULARY ☐ I can use collocations with nouns. (p. 49)

WRITING ☐ I can write a descriptive essay. (p. 51)

GRAMMAR ☐ I can use definite and indefinite articles. (p. 57)

OBJECTIVE ▶ ☐ I can gather information and ideas to write a descriptive essay about an advertisement for a product, business, or service.

Developmental Psychology

What important lessons do we learn as young people?

A. Discuss these questions with your classmates.

1. Who were your friends when you were growing up? What activities did you participate in?

2. What are some life lessons you learned from your parents?

3. Look at the photo. How do you think the people feel?

B. Listen to *The Q Classroom* online. Then answer these questions.

1. What important lessons did Felix, Sophy, and Yuna learn as young people? What is one lesson you learned?

2. What does Marcus say about learning from our parents? Sophy disagrees with Marcus. Who do you agree with? Why?

iQ PRACTICE Go to the online discussion board to discuss the Unit Question with your classmates. *Practice > Unit 3 > Activity 1*

UNIT OBJECTIVE

Read a magazine article and a blog post. Gather information and ideas to write a narrative essay about someone or something that influenced you when you were younger.

READING 1

The Difference Between Fitting in and Belonging, and Why It Matters

OBJECTIVE ▶

You are going to read a magazine article about fitting in and belonging. Use the article to gather information and ideas for your Unit Assignment.

PREVIEW THE READING

A. PREVIEW Read the title. Look at the photograph. What do you think the title means by *fitting in*? What about *belonging*?

B. QUICK WRITE What decisions did you make as a young person about your appearance, activities, and time? For example, what did you wear? What activities and groups did you participate in? How did you spend your free time? Write for 5–10 minutes in response. Remember to use this section for your Unit Assignment.

C. VOCABULARY Check (✓) the words you know. Use a dictionary to define any new or unknown words. Then discuss with a partner how the words will relate to the unit.

anxiety *(n.)* 🔑+ OPAL	fit in *(v. phr.)*
barrier *(n.)* 🔑+ OPAL	foundation *(n.)* 🔑+
coping *(n.)* 🔑+	negotiate *(v.)* 🔑+
courage *(n.)* 🔑+	self-fulfillment *(n.)*
empathy *(n.)*	shame *(n.)* 🔑+
extensive *(adj.)* 🔑+ OPAL	

🔑+ Oxford 5000™ words   OPAL Oxford Phrasal Academic Lexicon

iQ PRACTICE   Go online to listen and practice your pronunciation.
Practice ＞ Unit 3 ＞ Activity 2

A. INVESTIGATE Read the article and gather information about the important lessons we learn as young people.

THE DIFFERENCE BETWEEN FITTING IN AND BELONGING, AND WHY IT MATTERS

1 We all want to **fit in**, don't we? I remember how painful middle school was because my parents couldn't or wouldn't buy me the "cool" clothes for school that the popular kids were wearing. We were much too frugal for that in our family. I was never one of the popular kids. Maybe those clothes would have helped, but in truth, I probably never would have been a popular kid anyway. I made friends and formed connections with kids who didn't care about popularity or cool clothes. Some of those people are still my friends today.

2 Which brings me to the topics of fitting in versus belonging, and how we can get there from here.

FITTING IN VS. BELONGING

3 We all feel the need to be part of social groups in our communities, and we all make choices that affect the connections we make to others. At a young age, we begin to make decisions about our appearance, our social activities, and our time commitments. We choose how we look—our hair, our clothes, and even what we do to our bodies—who we hang out with, and how we spend our time. In making these choices, we may either be trying to fit in or to belong. Brene Brown, PhD, a social scientist and research professor, has been doing **extensive** research over the past 17 years on what she calls our "inextricable[1] human connections" and on true belonging. "The greatest **barrier** to belonging," she says, "is fitting in." So what are the differences between fitting in and belonging?

4 According to Brown, fitting in is changing ourselves to match the situation. In other words, fitting in is doing what is "cool." For example, it is wearing the right clothes, playing the most popular sport, or hanging out with the "best" social groups. But fitting in may cause feelings of **anxiety** or loneliness. Fitting in is easier in the sense that you don't have to go against the norm. However, according to Brown, it is **shame**-based and sends messages, especially to young people, that they are not good enough. As we work to conform to the expectations of others, we lose the sense of belonging to our real selves. Why? Brown says that we have a deep fear that if we present our authentic selves, we won't be liked. In addition, young people who feel pressured to fit in in ways that aren't healthy to their overall identities may end up participating in unhealthy relationships or going along with the crowd. Worse, they might begin participating in hurtful or mean-spirited behaviors, including bullying.

---

[1] **inextricable:** too closely linked to be separated

Fitting in or belonging?

5   Belonging is something else. It is letting ourselves be seen and known as we really are—being our true or authentic selves. It is wearing clothing that makes us feel good or that allows us to show our uniqueness, doing activities we enjoy, and spending time with people we can be our authentic selves with. Belonging brings enjoyment, excitement, or **self-fulfillment**. But it doesn't come easy. Being different can make us feel vulnerable—exposed to emotional uncertainty and risk. But, Brown claims, it's this same vulnerability that becomes the **foundation** on which **courage** is built. These findings surprised even Brown. She had assumed that belonging was external—that people **negotiated** with the groups they want to join. Instead, she found that the people with the deepest sense of belonging are those who have the courage to stand alone and risk being disconnected from others.

[2] **resilient:** able to feel better quickly after something unpleasant such as a shock, injury, etc.

HOW TO GET FROM HERE TO THERE

6   Belonging matters because it is important to healthy human development. We all need to feel like we are connected to people and groups. We seek love, acceptance, and connection. We want to feel valued, needed, cared for, and appreciated. Humans who belong are more resilient[2].

7   So how do we get there? Here are three key features of belonging: connecting, caring, and **coping**. Connecting is the experience of having meaningful bonds with others. Caring involves developing **empathy** for others, especially across differences. It helps us deepen connections to others who may also need support in belonging. And coping, according to Kenneth Ginsburg, M.D., a professor of pediatrics, is the act of being resilient in the face of stress, including the pressure to fit in. Developing these three features can help us all find our way along the path to belonging.

VOCABULARY SKILL REVIEW

In Unit 2, you learned that there are common collocations with nouns. What three nouns in the Activity B word box can follow *feel?* What verb + noun collocations can you think of?

B. VOCABULARY Complete each sentence with the vocabulary from Reading 1.

anxiety *(n.)*	courage *(n.)*	fit in *(v. phr.)*	self-fulfillment *(n.)*
barrier *(n.)*	empathy *(n.)*	foundation *(n.)*	shame *(n.)*
coping *(n.)*	extensive *(adj.)*	negotiate *(v.)*	

1. They truly understood the feelings of the boy who was being bullied and felt great _____ for him.

2. I wanted to _____ so badly that I was willing to do things I shouldn't have.

3. It's normal to worry and experience _____ when in a new social situation.

4. He found _____ in his work and was satisfied with the career path he had chosen.

5. She showed a lot of _____ when she chose to pursue her dream to write poetry, even though she risked being bullied because of her choice.

6. For the group to reach an agreement, the members had to _____ a decision that was satisfactory to all of them.

7. Because she is an expert, her knowledge is _____.

8. Lack of money is often the _____ that prevents a young person from getting a college education.

9. When he wasn't chosen for the team, he felt _____ that he wasn't good enough.

10. _____ is an important life skill needed to deal with life's challenges.

11. A good friendship is based on a(n) _____ of shared interests.

iQ PRACTICE   Go online for more practice with the vocabulary.
Practice > Unit 3 > Activity 3

C. EXPLAIN Answer the questions.

1. What is the main idea of the reading? _____

   _____

2. What is one important difference between fitting in and belonging?

   _____

3. Explain one of these ideas: connecting, caring, and coping.

   _____

D. IDENTIFY Circle the correct answer.

1. What is the purpose of the first paragraph?

   a. It gives a definition of the topic of the article.

   b. It gives a solution to the topic of the article.

   c. It gives an example of the topic of the article.

2. What is the topic of paragraph 3?

   a. decisions about our appearance

   b. choices we make

   c. social groups

3. Fitting in is ____ while belonging is ____.

   a. changing ourselves / being ourselves

   b. wanting to be fulfilled / wanting to be accepted

   c. having courage / feeling uncomfortable

4. What is one possible result of trying to fit in rather than belong?

   a. We are vulnerable.

   b. We participate in hurtful activities.

   c. We are authentic.

5. The audience of this article is probably ____.

   a. young people experiencing bullying

   b. researchers specializing in adult anxiety

   c. readers interested in psychology

6. The conclusion of this reading is: ____.

   a. We can all belong.

   b. We have to learn to cope with life.

   c. It's stressful to fit in.

E. CATEGORIZE Read the statements. Write *T* (true) or *F* (false) and the paragraph number where the answer is found. Then correct each false statement to make it true according to the article.

____ 1. The author didn't make friends in middle school. (paragraph ____)

____ 2. Fitting in is wearing clothes so others will accept us. (paragraph ____)

____ 3. Belonging is participating in activities, so we won't be lonely. (paragraph ____)

____ 4. According to Brene Brown, we change ourselves to belong. (paragraph ____)

____ 5. Fitting in is hard because we are going with the norm. (paragraph ____)

____ 6. People who allow themselves to be vulnerable have courage. (paragraph ____)

____ 7. People with a sense of belonging stay true to what they believe. (paragraph ____)

____ 8. We should help young people learn how to fit in. (paragraph ____)

F. CATEGORIZE Complete the chart with information from the reading. Compare charts with a partner. Discuss where in the reading you found the information and why you have the opinions you do.

	Fitting in	Belonging
is		
is doing		
is wearing		
is being		
makes us		
in my opinion is		

G. SYNTHESIZE Look back at your Quick Write on page 64. What decisions did you make as a young person about your appearance, activities, and time? Add any new ideas or information you learned from the reading.

iQ PRACTICE Go online for additional reading and comprehension.
Practice > Unit 3 > Activity 4

WRITE WHAT YOU THINK

A. DISCUSS Discuss the questions in a group. Think about the Unit Question, "What important lessons do we learn as young people?"

1. Can you think of a time when you were happy to fit in? Can you think of a time when you did not want to just fit it?

2. The article says that "the people with the deepest sense of belonging are those who have the courage to stand alone." What do you think that means?

3. Who are you with when you feel that you really belong? Why is that?

B. SYNTHESIZE Choose one of the questions from Activity A and write a paragraph of 5–7 sentences in response. Look back at your Quick Write on page 64 as you think about what you learned.

 CRITICAL THINKING STRATEGY

Relating to the reading

The following activity asks you to **relate** the information in the article to your own life. When you connect new information to your own experience, you deepen your understanding of it. When you read, ask yourself how the information applies to you.

> **The author says:** We all feel the need to be part of social groups in our communities.
>
> **The reader says:** I am a part of my family, my neighborhood, my group of friends, and my school tennis team.

iQ PRACTICE Go online to watch the Critical Thinking Video and check your comprehension. *Practice > Unit 3 > Activity 5*

C. APPLY Read these sentences from Reading 1. Write how each relates to you. Use examples from your own experience. Discuss your ideas with a partner.

1. Fitting in is changing ourselves to match the situation.

_____

2. Belonging . . . is letting ourselves be seen and known as we really are.

_____

3. Being different can make us feel vulnerable . . . it's this same vulnerability that becomes the foundation on which courage is built.

_____

4. Young people who feel pressured to fit in . . . may end up participating in unhealthy relationships.

_____

Writers don't usually state all their ideas directly. Usually, they expect the reader to **infer** some ideas that the information suggests. Making inferences about a text means that you use your knowledge to make a logical conclusion about the information that is given. Look at this excerpt from Reading 1.

> Brene Brown, PhD, a social scientist and research professor, has been doing extensive research over the past 17 years on what she calls our "inextricable human connections" and on true belonging.

You can infer:

- Brene Brown has the training and the knowledge to conduct and evaluate research.

- She is very interested in human connections and true belonging.

Making inferences helps you improve your comprehension and understand a text more deeply.

TIP FOR SUCCESS

Your inferences should always depend on the author's words first and your experience second. Make sure your inferences are not contradicted by statements that are made later in the text.

A. INTERPRET Read the paragraph from Reading 1. Check (✓) the statements that can be inferred from the text. Then compare answers with a partner. Explain what information in the paragraph led to the inference.

> We all feel the need to be part of social groups in our communities, and we all make choices that affect the connections we make to others. At a young age, we begin to make decisions about our appearance, our social activities, and our time commitments. We choose how we look—our hair, our clothes, and even what we do to our bodies—who we hang out with, and how we spend our time. In making these choices, we may either be trying to fit in or to belong.

- ☐ 1. Connecting with others is part of being human.
- ☐ 2. We continue making decisions about fitting in when we are adults.
- ☐ 3. We might cut our hair in order to fit in.
- ☐ 4. The need to be part of a group is not universal.
- ☐ 5. Our social activities include who we hang out with.
- ☐ 6. Fitting in and belonging are the same thing.

B. INTERPRET Read the paragraph. Make inferences. You may circle *a*, *b*, or both. Then compare answers with a partner. Explain your answers.

> I have always had to struggle to get out of bed in the morning. When I was a young child, the problem wasn't so bad. Because I didn't want to miss anything that my older siblings were doing, I made myself get up. But as each one of them went away to college, I had less and less enthusiasm for getting up in the mornings. After they were all gone, my father used to come to my bedroom door, knock, and say, "It's 6:00. Wake up and get out of bed." I would respond, "One or the other, Dad. One or the other."

1. The writer ____.

   a. had four older siblings

   b. was the youngest child

2. The writer ____.

   a. still struggles to get out of bed

   b. got out of bed easily as a young child

3. The writer's father ____.

   a. used to get up early

   b. would get annoyed

4. The writer's response to the father suggests the writer ____.

   a. has a good sense of humor

   b. would get up right away

iQ PRACTICE Go online for more practice making inferences.
Practice › Unit 3 › Activity 6

READING 2

Life Lessons I Learned from My Dad in 23 Years

OBJECTIVE ▶

You are going to read a blog post by Katie Hurley, child and adolescent psychotherapist and author of articles and books on parenting. She writes about the things she learned from her father, who died when she was 23. Use the blog post to gather ideas and information for your Unit Assignment.

PREVIEW THE READING

A. PREVIEW Read the title and answer the first question. Then read the paragraph headings and answer the second question.

1. What life lessons will Katie Hurley discuss? Predict three.

2. Do your predictions match any of the headings?

B. QUICK WRITE Who influenced you most as an adult? Write for 5–10 minutes in response. Be sure to use this section for your Unit Assignment.

C. VOCABULARY Check (✓) the words you know. Use a dictionary to define any new or unknown words. Then discuss with a partner how the words will relate to the unit.

attribute *(v.)* ⁺ OPAL	intervention *(n.)* ⁺ OPAL	tragic *(adj.)* ⁺
encounter *(v.)* ⁺ OPAL	petrified *(adj.)*	void *(n.)*
hesitation *(n.)*	pitch in *(v. phr.)*	work ethic *(n. phr.)*
interaction *(n.)* ⁺ OPAL	refrain *(n.)*	wounded *(adj.)* ⁺

⁺ Oxford 5000™ words   **OPAL** Oxford Phrasal Academic Lexicon

iQ PRACTICE   Go online to listen and practice your pronunciation.
Practice › Unit 3 › Activity 7

WORK WITH THE READING

A. INVESTIGATE Read the blog post and gather information about the important lessons we learn as young people.

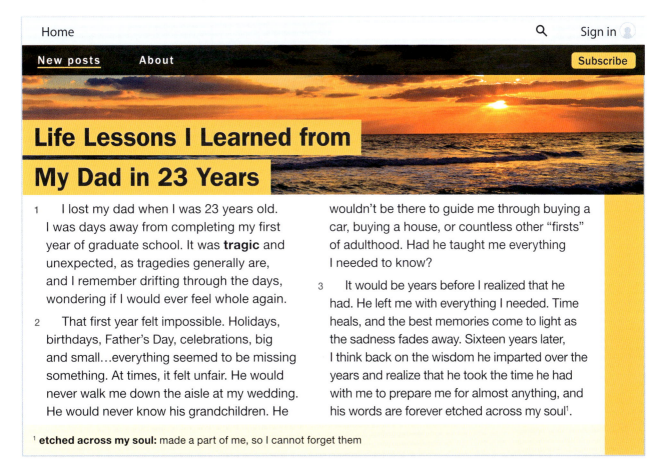

Home   🔍   Sign in 👤

New posts   About   Subscribe

Life Lessons I Learned from
My Dad in 23 Years

1   I lost my dad when I was 23 years old. I was days away from completing my first year of graduate school. It was **tragic** and unexpected, as tragedies generally are, and I remember drifting through the days, wondering if I would ever feel whole again.

2   That first year felt impossible. Holidays, birthdays, Father's Day, celebrations, big and small…everything seemed to be missing something. At times, it felt unfair. He would never walk me down the aisle at my wedding. He would never know his grandchildren. He wouldn't be there to guide me through buying a car, buying a house, or countless other "firsts" of adulthood. Had he taught me everything I needed to know?

3   It would be years before I realized that he had. He left me with everything I needed. Time heals, and the best memories come to light as the sadness fades away. Sixteen years later, I think back on the wisdom he imparted over the years and realize that he took the time he had with me to prepare me for almost anything, and his words are forever etched across my soul[1].

---
[1] **etched across my soul:** made a part of me, so I cannot forget them

4 **1 Family consists of the relationships you choose to nurture.**

Life is hard, and families can be complicated. My dad's story isn't mine to tell, but his family changed over time. As an adolescent, I questioned him about these changes. Did he miss the people he no longer saw?

5 His answer was simple: "This is my family. Your family is made up of the people you love, and the people who love you back. That's all you need."

6 **2 Kindness counts.**

When people recall their memories of my dad they often refer to him as friendly, kind, and generous. They talk about long boat rides and the fact that he was always willing to **pitch in** and lend a hand.

7 I know he secretly lived in fear that I would bring home every **wounded** bird I **encountered**. I was always trying to help. As much as some might say that can be **attributed** to personality, I like to think that some of it came from my parents. They taught me to be kind and help out when I can, and I teach my children the same.

8 **3 Bravery happens when you're ready to be brave.**

I was **petrified** of my dad's boat when I was young. It was loud and stinky and made a horrible cracking sound each time he took a wave. My brother loved it. I cried every time they strapped the life jacket on me. For four years, I never even made it out of the lagoon.

9 I knew his boat was important to him. Kids know things. And I wanted to love that boat just as much as everyone else. So at the end of my fourth summer, I made an announcement: "When I'm five, I'll be brave." For that entire winter following my fifth birthday, I bravely chanted that **refrain**. And when the boat showed up in the garage that spring, the anxiety set in. Sensing my **hesitation**, my dad leaned down and whispered, "You don't have to be brave this year. You can be brave when you're ready."

10 I never forgot that **interaction**. When I stepped off the dock and onto the boat that summer, I stood tall and smiled. And I loved every second of it.

11 **4 Hard work will get you everywhere.**

I was always the kind of student who wanted to get straight As and cried when a B+ showed up on my report, so I never needed any **intervention** when it came to school. But my dad noticed my hard work. He frequently complimented my writing and my focus and reminded me that my **work ethic** would help me reach my goals. All of them. As it turns out, he was right.

5 **It's OK to walk away sometimes.**

12   There was one summer when my dad was reading the most boring book of all time. It just sat on the coffee table for days at a time. Occasionally, he would pick it up and read a few pages, only to return to the newspaper. I finally asked him about it. "Sometimes things aren't what they seem, Kate. It's important to know when to walk away. I'm walking away from this one."

13   I'm not a quitter by nature, but I have walked away from a couple of things that weren't as they seemed. And I've never once regretted a decision to leave something behind.

6 **If you can count your friends on two hands, you're good².**

14   Adolescence was torture at times. I never knew where I fit in. My best friend went off to boarding school, and I couldn't quite fill the **void**. I was sobbing over my outcast status³ when my dad presented me with this little nugget of wisdom⁴ one night. I didn't believe him at the time, but I've seen the light⁵. I can count my friends on two hands.

7 **Every sunset has meaning.**

15   My dad loved a sunset. He was most at peace with himself at our house by the beach, and he never missed a sunset during the summer months. It was the summer before his death that I asked him what he loved about sunsets.

16   This is what he said: "If you've had a rotten day, a sunset reminds you that another day is ahead. If you've had a great day, a sunset reminds you to soak it in⁶. Either way, it's a win."

8 **Life is short; make it count.**

17   Fifty-two years doesn't seem like enough, and yet that's what he had. I believe that my dad did the best that he could with the time he had.

18   If nothing else, he always encouraged me to just be me. "At the end of the line, you only have who you are. Be the best version of you. People will respect you for it."

---

² **you're good:** it's OK; it's a good thing
³ **outcast status:** not belonging to the group; not having friends
⁴ **nugget of wisdom:** piece of important information
⁵ **see the light:** to understand
⁶ **soak it in:** spend time experiencing and enjoying; like **soak it up:** absorb into your senses

B. VOCABULARY Here are some words from Reading 2. Read the sentences. Then write each bold word next to the correct definition on page 76. You may need to change the form of some of the words.

1. We were very sad to hear about the **tragic** accident.

2. If everyone **pitches in**, the work will be done very soon.

3. The **wounded** bicyclist was taken to the hospital to treat his injuries.

4. I **encountered** my neighbors at the community picnic.

5. His success can be **attributed** to his hard work.

6. The young boy was **petrified** by the large angry dog running toward him.

7. He kept repeating the **refrain** over and over to help himself remember it.

8. Her **hesitation** was a result of her feelings of uncertainty.

9. We had a very pleasant **interaction** with them at the meeting.

10. Their quick **intervention** helped save the child from harm.

11. There was nothing there in the **void**.

12. A strong **work ethic** will always help you do well in any job.

a. _____ (v.) to say something is the result of a particular thing

b. _____ (adj.) extremely frightened

c. _____ (n.) the act of being slow to speak or act because you feel uncertain or nervous

d. _____ (n.) action taken to improve or help a situation

e. _____ (v. phr.) to join in and help with an activity, by doing some of the work

f. _____ (n.) a belief in work as a moral good

g. _____ (n.) a large empty space

h. _____ (v.) to meet, run into

i. _____ (adj.) making you feel very sad, usually because someone has died

j. _____ (n.) the act of communicating with someone

k. _____ (n.) a comment or statement that is often repeated

l. _____ (adj.) injured as in an accident

iQ PRACTICE   Go online for more practice with the vocabulary.
Practice > Unit 3 > Activity 8

C. **IDENTIFY** Each of these sentences gives a main idea of a lesson that Katie Hurley learned from her dad. Write the correct lesson number next to each sentence.

1. Enjoying nature is a good way to end each day. ____

2. When the time is right, you can be brave. ____

3. If something isn't right, it's OK to quit. ____

4. Be kind and help others. ____

5. Be true to yourself. ____

6. Working hard is important. ____

7. Your family is the people you care about. ____

8. A few good friends are enough. ____

D. EXPLAIN Answer the questions about Katie Hurley and her father.

1. How old was she when her father died?

   _____

2. What was she doing when her father died?

   _____

3. How much time has passed since her father died?

   _____

4. What has her father missed in her life?

   _____

5. How old was her father when he died?

   _____

6. What time of day did her father like best?

   _____

7. Why did her father quit reading the book?

   _____

8. How do other people remember her father?

   _____

E. CATEGORIZE Check (✓) the statements you can infer about Katie Hurley and her father based on the blog post.

Katie Hurley	Her father
☐ She is successful.	☐ He was friendly.
☐ She misses her father.	☐ He had a successful career.
☐ She learned a lot from her father.	☐ He liked the water.
☐ She was a happy adolescent.	☐ He was a good father.
☐ She loves the water.	☐ He liked to fish.
☐ She is brave.	☐ He died in an accident.

F. EXTEND Work with a partner. Find a sentence in the blog post to support the statements you checked in Activity E. Discuss why you didn't check the other statements.

WORK WITH THE VIDEO

A. PREVIEW Have you ever quit doing an activity? Why?

VIDEO VOCABULARY

instill (v.) to make someone feel a particular way over time

pick on (v.) to treat unfairly by blaming, criticizing, or punishing

self-esteem (n.) a feeling of being happy with your own character and abilities

rule of thumb (n.) a practical method of measuring something, usually based on past experience

stamina (n.) physical or mental strength that enables you to do something for long periods

iQ **RESOURCES** Go online to watch the video about children who want to quit doing an activity. *Resources > Video > Unit 3 > Unit Video*

B. COMPOSE Watch the video two or three times. Take notes in the first part of the chart.

	Reasons children quit	Ways to help children commit
Notes from the video		
My ideas		

C. EXTEND Why else do children quit? What are some other ways parents can help children commit to activities? Write your ideas in the chart above. Discuss your ideas with a partner.

WRITE WHAT YOU THINK

SYNTHESIZE Think about Reading 1, Reading 2, and the unit video as you discuss these questions. Then choose one question and write a paragraph of 5–7 sentences in response.

1. Number 6 of Ms. Hurley's list of lessons talks about fitting in. How does the idea of counting your friends on two hands illustrate the idea of belonging?

2. Choose one of the tips from Reading 2 (besides number 6). Explain how this tip also is about belonging instead of fitting in.

3. Think about what you have read and watched about caring and coping. Who in your life helped you learn to connect, care, and cope? Give examples.

VOCABULARY SKILL Prefixes and suffixes

A **prefix** is a group of letters that comes at the beginning of a word. When you add a prefix to a word, it usually changes the word's meaning.

Prefix	Meaning	Example
anti-	against	antiwar
co-	together	cooperation
extra-	more	extracurricular
in-	not	independence
inter-	go between	interaction
mid-	middle	mid-fifties
mis-	incorrect, badly	misunderstanding
re-	again	reread

A **suffix** is a group of letters that comes at the end of a word. When you add a suffix to a word, it usually changes the part of speech of that word. For example, adding the suffix *-tion* to the verb *inform* makes it the noun *information*.

ACADEMIC LANGUAGE
The corpus shows that *the significance of* is often used in academic writing.
. . . the significance of Dr. Brown's research . . .
. . . the significance of the parents' actions . . .

OPAL
Oxford Phrasal Academic Lexicon

Suffixes that form nouns	-ence / -ance	competence, significance
	-tion	foundation, connection
Suffixes that form adjectives	-ent / -ant	consistent, important
	-ful	resentful, meaningful
Suffixes that form verbs	-ate	investigate, motivate
	-ize	organize, realize

iQ PRACTICE Go online to watch the the Vocabulary Skill video.
Resources > Video > Unit 3 > Vocabulary Skill Video

A. APPLY Complete the word in each sentence with the correct prefix from the Vocabulary Skill chart on page 79. Then check your answers in the dictionary.

1. He _____ pronounced the word, so she didn't understand what he had said.

2. They were both _____ ordinary students. They excelled at school and were talented in sports and poetry as well.

3. Many parts of the brain are _____ connected. They work together to enable the brain's many functions.

4. His job required that he _____ locate often, so he had lived in many places.

5. Fatimah knew she wasn't ready for _____ term exams, but she hoped she'd do better on the final.

6. People assumed Ali was _____ social because he rarely spoke with other children.

7. Some siblings have to learn to _____ exist peacefully with each other.

8. We're going to have a(n) _____ formal gathering tonight. Come by if you want.

B. IDENTIFY Read each word. Check (✓) the correct part of speech. Use information from the Vocabulary Skill box on page 79 to help you. Then check your answers in the dictionary.

	Noun	Adjective	Verb
1. recognize	☐	☐	☐
2. reliance	☐	☐	☐
3. peaceful	☐	☐	☐
4. demonstrate	☐	☐	☐
5. resilient	☐	☐	☐
6. contribution	☐	☐	☐
7. confidence	☐	☐	☐
8. significant	☐	☐	☐
9. substance	☐	☐	☐
10. negotiate	☐	☐	☐
11. imagination	☐	☐	☐
12. cheerful	☐	☐	☐

C. COMPOSE Choose five words from Activity B. Write a sentence for each.

iQ PRACTICE Go online for more practice with prefixes and suffixes.
Practice > Unit 3 > Activity 9

WRITING

At the end of this unit, you will write a narrative essay about someone or something that influenced you when you were younger. This essay will include specific information from the readings, the unit video, and your own ideas.

WRITING SKILL Writing a narrative essay and varying sentence patterns

A **narrative essay** tells a story about a personal experience, event, or memory.

Organization

- The **introduction** sets the scene for the reader. It should give information about the people, place, and time, and should create interest in the story. The introduction may include a **thesis statement** that tells why the story is important or memorable.

- There can be one or more **body paragraphs**. These tell the main events or actions of the story. They are usually in the order in which the events happened. They may also include important or interesting details to support the ideas in the main event.

- The **conclusion** gives the outcome or result of the actions in the story. It often tells what the writer learned from the experience.

Expressing the order of events

In a narrative essay, you use **time phrases** and **clauses** to explain when the events happened in the story and the order of events.

> **Prepositional phrases: in** 1978, **on** June 5, **before/after** class, **for** five years
>
> **Time expressions:** a week **ago**, **last** month, **earlier** this year, the week **before**, an hour **later**, the **next** day
>
> **Time clauses: after** we spoke, **before** I ate, **as** they were leaving, **when** we met

Varying sentence patterns

Varying sentence patterns in your writing will help the reader maintain interest and focus on important information. Here are some ways to add variety to your writing.

- Shorter sentences emphasize or stress one important point.

- Longer sentences combine closely related ideas. Longer sentences can be made by using conjunctions, subordinators, or relative clauses to combine shorter sentences.

> | | |
> |---|---|
> | **Shorter:** | There was a sudden noise. |
> | **Longer** (with conjunction): | Then a cat jumped out of the bushes **and** ran up the path. |
> | **Longer** (with subordinator): | **Even though** it was only a cat, my heart started beating faster. |
> | **Longer** (with relative clause): | The next noise **that I heard** was definitely not a cat. |

A. CREATE Brainstorm ideas for a narrative essay.

1. Draw a timeline of four or five events that you remember from your childhood. Put on your timeline how old you were and a short phrase indicating what happened. Look at the example.

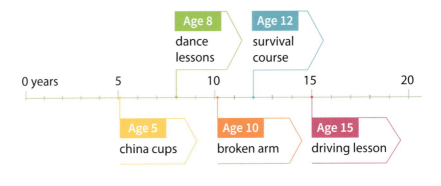

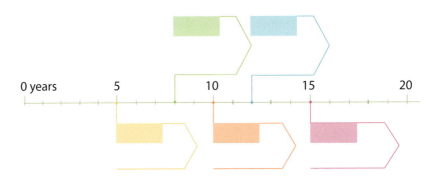

WRITING TIP
Using a **timeline** is a good way to plan a narrative essay. A timeline can help you map out important events in the order in which they occurred.

2. Choose one of the events on your timeline and answer these questions.

   a. What happened?

   _____

   b. Who was with you?

   _____

   c. Where were you?

   _____

   d. When did it happen?

   _____

   e. What did you learn?

   _____

B. WRITING MODEL Read the model narrative essay. Notice the organizational structure. Then answer the questions that follow.

My Mother's China Cups

introduction

1   When I think about my mother, one thing I remember is her collection of china cups and saucers. She had collected them throughout her life, and they were very important to her. They were displayed on shelves in our kitchen. Some of them were quite old; some she had gotten from faraway places. And each one had a special memory for her.

body paragraph 1

2   From a very young age, I always wanted to take down those beautiful cups and wash them. It was my chance to see them up close. My mother never really wanted to let me do it. She knew the cups were fragile and I could easily break them. But sometimes I begged until she let me take them down and clean them.

body paragraph 2

3   My earliest memory of this was when I was five. I pulled a chair near the kitchen table and took down the small cups. I started with my favorites: the very old blue and white one that had belonged to my great-grandmother and the one from Japan with exotic buildings on it. I moved them all, one by one, to the kitchen counter. After I had put them on the counter, I moved my chair to the sink, filled the sink with soapy water, and began to wash the tiny cups.

body paragraph 3

4   I had only washed a few when the beautiful blue and white cup slipped from my small hands and fell back into the sink. The handle broke off. My mother's special cup was ruined, and I was sure she would be angry. I cried and waited for quite a while before I could find the courage to tell her. My mother, who was probably upset, only smiled and said we would glue it back together. I happily finished washing the precious cups. When I had cleaned and dried them all, we carefully placed them back on the shelves. Then my mother glued the handle back on the broken cup before we set it back in its place, too.

conclusion

5   I washed those cups many times as a child, and almost every time, I broke one. By the time I was grown, several showed the signs of my efforts. I am an adult now and my mother is gone, but I will always remember that she cared more about encouraging me than about her valuable cups. Now, as a mother myself, I understand the patience it took to allow me to handle her precious things. I try to demonstrate that same level of caring to my own children.

1. Who are the people in the narrative?

   _____

2. Where does the action take place?

   _____

3. When does the action take place?

   _____

C. RESTATE Complete the outline of the essay. You do not have to use the writer's exact words.

   I. Introductory ideas: _____

    _____

WRITING TIP
When writing a narrative, use details and descriptive language to make the story come alive for the reader. See the Writing Skill on page 51 for more information.

  II. Body paragraph 1: Main event in story

    When I was a child, I always wanted to wash my mother's china cups.

    A. Important or interesting detail: _____

    _____

    B. Important or interesting detail: _____

    _____

  III. Body paragraph 2: Main event in story

    _____

    A. Important or interesting detail: *I started with my favorites—*

    the old blue and white one and the one from Japan.

    B. Important or interesting detail: _____

    _____

  IV. Body paragraph 3: Main event in story

    _____

    A. Important or interesting detail: _____

    _____

    B. Important or interesting detail: *My mother glued the handle on*

    the cup before we put it back on the shelf.

  V. Conclusion (what I learned): _____

    _____

D. IDENTIFY Look at body paragraph 3 of "My Mother's China Cups" on page 83. Circle the conjunctions. Underline the subordinators. Put a star (*) next to the relative clause. Then answer these questions.

1. Write the shortest sentence here. _____

2. How many conjunctions did you find? ____

3. How many subordinators? ____

4. The relative clause has commas around it. Who does the relative clause describe? _____

TIP FOR SUCCESS

You do not have to use all the techniques in everything you write. Just be sure to vary the patterns that you use.

E. RESTATE Work with a partner to rewrite the paragraph below. Vary the sentence patterns by keeping some shorter sentences and by using conjunctions, subordinators, and relative clauses to make longer sentences.

> The toughest weekend of my life was also one of the best. I was 12. My father and I attended a short survival course. I will never forget it. I woke up early on a Saturday morning. It was still dark. I wanted to go back to sleep. My father was wide awake. My father was excited about the day ahead. We ate a quick breakfast. We drove to the school at the edge of the desert. We arrived at 7 a.m. The desert was already hot. I felt nervous. I didn't want to show it. The other students arrived. One was a boy. He was about my age. He was with his father, too. The instructor came out to greet us.

Example: The toughest weekend of my life was also one of the best. When I was 12, my father and I attended a short survival course that I will never forget. . . .

F. IDENTIFY Go back to your paragraph from Activity E. Circle the conjunctions. Underline the subordinators. Put a star (*) next to the relative clauses. Then answer these questions.

1. How many short sentences do you have? ____

2. How many sentences have conjunctions? ____

3. How many sentences have subordinators? ____

4. How many sentences have relative clauses? ____

G. IDENTIFY Read the rest of the essay from Activity E. Choose one of the paragraphs in the essay. Circle the conjunctions. Underline the subordinators. Put a star (*) next to the relative clauses.

> The instructor—a tall, athletic man—looked at us seriously. "You are going to learn about survival," he said. "This may be the most challenging and rewarding weekend of your life." I looked at my father. I wasn't sure that I wanted to continue, but he was still very excited. "You will learn how to do such things as find food, find shelter, and keep warm. I won't tell you that it is going to be easy. In fact, it won't be. However, at the end of the weekend, I hope you'll think that it was worth the effort."

❯ *continued on page 86*

We set out with only our water bottles and knives. We hiked through the desert for miles in the hot sun. I was afraid that we would run out of water, but our guide said that we would be fine as long as we didn't waste any. Along the way, we looked for food. We found an edible plant that people call a barrel cactus. We also caught a lizard that people can boil and eat, but no one wanted to. We were hungry and tired when the instructor had us stop near some flowering cactus. We ate the flowers, which tasted OK, and we rested in the shade of some large rocks.

I don't remember much about the rest of the first day, but I do remember that the air got cold quickly when the sun set and I was happy to sit close to my father, near the fire that we had helped build. I looked up at the stars and smiled. They were so beautiful, out away from the city. I looked up at my father and saw his face more peaceful than I could remember ever seeing it before.

It was a tough weekend, but I am glad we went. I learned about the desert and how to survive in it, but more importantly, I learned about myself and my father. We had shared a difficult time in the desert, and we grew closer because of it. Long afterward, whenever we saw the stars, one or the other would say, "Remember that night in the desert?" and we would both smile.

iQ PRACTICE   Go online for more practice with writing narrative essays and varying sentence patterns. *Practice > Unit 3 > Activity 10*

GRAMMAR Past perfect and past perfect continuous

Order of events in the past

The **past perfect** shows that one event happened before another event in the past. The past perfect expresses the earlier event. The simple past is often used to express the later event. The past perfect often gives background information about events or situations. It has the same form for all subjects: subject + *had* (+ *not*) + past participle.

Past perfect with past time clauses

The past perfect is often used in sentences with **past time clauses**. A past time clause usually begins with a subordinator such as *when*, *until*, or *by the time*. Notice the use of a comma when the past time clause comes first.

Past perfect continuous

The **past perfect continuous** is used for actions that began in the past and continued up to another past event or state in the past. It is often used with *for* to indicate how long a situation lasted. Like the past perfect, it often gives background information. The past perfect continuous is subject + *had* + *been* + verb + *-ing*.

I **had been living** there for six months when the Smiths moved next door.

She **had been writing** stories for many years when her first story was published.

When she finally arrived, he'**d been waiting** for her for two hours.

A. **IDENTIFY** Read the sentences. Underline the past perfect and past perfect continuous verbs and circle the simple past verbs in each example. Label the verbs *1* for the earlier event and *2* for the later event.

1. My mother had a collection of very small china cups and saucers.
   She had collected them throughout her life.

2. I had only washed a few when the beautiful blue and white cup slipped from my small hands.

3. I had forgotten to call my brother, so he was angry with me.

4. She had thought seriously about studying medicine, but in the end, she decided to study business.

5. Until he got an internship at a big ad agency, he hadn't been interested in working in advertising.

6. I didn't answer the man because I hadn't heard him clearly.

7. We had been working on the project for hours when we finally finished it.

B. RESTATE Combine the sentences using the time expression indicated. Change the simple past verb to the past perfect or past perfect continuous for the event that happened first. The sentences are in the order that they happened.

1. She was studying English. She moved to the United States. (when)

   _____

2. I did not leave my home country. I visited Canada. (until)

   _____

3. He already finished reading the book. He watched the movie. (when)

   _____

4. They recalled important events from their past. The students wrote stories about their memories of childhood. (after)

   _____

   _____

5. I had lunch. She arrived at the restaurant. (by the time)

   _____

6. I offered to pay for lunch. I realized that I didn't have any money. (when)

   _____

iQ PRACTICE Go online for more practice with the past perfect and past perfect continuous. *Practice > Unit 3 > Activities 11–12*

UNIT ASSIGNMENT Write a narrative essay

OBJECTIVE ▶

In this assignment, you are going to write a three-paragraph narrative essay about someone or something that influenced you when you were younger. As you prepare your essay, think about the Unit Question, "What important lessons do we learn as young people?" Use information from Reading 1, Reading 2, the unit video, and your work in this unit to support your essay. Refer to the Self-Assessment checklist on page 90.

iQ PRACTICE Go online to the Writing Tutor to read a model narrative essay. *Practice › Unit 3 › Activity 13*

PLAN AND WRITE

A. BRAINSTORM Follow these steps to help you organize your ideas.

1. Create a chart. Write down the names of some people or things that influenced you when you were younger.

TIP FOR SUCCESS

To help you remember all the details of your memory, ask and answer the six *wh-* questions: *who, what, where, when, why,* and *how.*

2. Think about memories associated with those people or things. Write notes about the memories and specific details such as people, times, and places. Look at the example.

	Memories	Details
People: My older brother	The time I fell off my bike when we were kids	I was 6. We were in Greenway Park. I cut my head. We went to see Dr. Garcia.
Things: Greenwich Elementary School	My first day of school	I was lost on my first day. Mrs. Lu found me on the school playground. She took me back to class.

B. PLAN Follow these steps to plan your essay.

1. Choose one of the people or things from Activity A to write about.

2. Circle the most interesting memories and the most important details.

iQ RESOURCES Go online to download and complete the outline for your narrative essay. *Resources › Writing Tools › Unit 3 › Outline*

C. WRITE Use your planning notes to write your essay.

1. To clearly express the order of the events, use time words and time clauses, the past perfect and past perfect continuous, and other past verb forms.

2. Look at the Self-Assessment checklist below to guide your writing.

iQ PRACTICE Go online to the Writing Tutor to write your assignment.
Practice > Unit 3 > Activity 14

REVISE AND EDIT

iQ RESOURCES Go online to download the peer review worksheet.
Resources > Writing Tools > Unit 3 > Peer Review Worksheet

A. PEER REVIEW Read your partner's essay. Then use the peer review worksheet. Discuss the review with your partner.

B. REVISE Based on your partner's review, revise and rewrite your essay.

C. EDIT Complete the Self-Assessment checklist as you prepare to write the final draft of your essay. Be prepared to hand in your work or discuss it in class.

SELF-ASSESSMENT	Yes	No
Does the introduction tell why the story is important?	☐	☐
Are the events in the order in which they happened?	☐	☐
Does the conclusion tell why the memory is important today?	☐	☐
Are time phrases and time clauses used to clearly express the order of the events?	☐	☐
Are the past perfect and past perfect continuous used appropriately to give background for other past events or situations?	☐	☐
Does the essay include vocabulary from the unit?	☐	☐
Did you check the essay for punctuation, spelling, and grammar?	☐	☐

D. REFLECT Discuss these questions with a partner or group.

1. What is something new you learned in this unit?

2. Look back at the Unit Question—What important lessons do we learn as young people? Is your answer different now than when you started the unit? If yes, how is it different? Why?

iQ PRACTICE Go to the online discussion board to discuss the questions.
Practice > Unit 3 > Activity 15

TRACK YOUR SUCCESS

iQ PRACTICE   Go online to check the words and phrases you have learned in this unit. *Practice › Unit 3 › Activity 16*

Check (✓) the skills and strategies you learned. If you need more work on a skill, refer to the page(s) in parentheses.

CRITICAL THINKING	☐ I can relate what the author writes to my own experience. (p. 70)
READING	☐ I can make inferences about a text. (p. 71)
VOCABULARY	☐ I can recognize and understand prefixes and suffixes. (p. 79)
WRITING	☐ I can organize and write a narrative essay and vary sentence patterns. (p. 81)
GRAMMAR	☐ I can understand and use the past perfect and past perfect continuous. (pp. 86–87)
OBJECTIVE ▶	☐ I can gather information and ideas to write a narrative essay about someone or something that influenced me when I was younger.

4 Science and Technology

CRITICAL THINKING	categorizing information
READING	understanding comparisons and contrasts
VOCABULARY	using the dictionary to distinguish between homonyms
WRITING	writing a compare and contrast essay
GRAMMAR	subordinators and transitions to compare and contrast

How can science improve lives?

A. Discuss these questions with your classmates.

1. Have you experienced a time without electricity? How did it affect your activities?

2. Which electronic device (an object or piece of equipment) would you miss the most if you didn't have it?

3. Look at the photo. What might the device do? How could it improve people's lives?

🔊 **B.** Listen to *The Q Classroom* online. Then answer these questions.

1. Marcus focuses on technology as one way that science can improve lives. What does Sophy focus on in her answer?

2. Yuna thinks that science sometimes doesn't help us and gives examples of air and water pollution. What is Felix's response to Yuna?

iQ PRACTICE Go to the online discussion board to discuss the Unit Question with your classmates. *Practice › Unit 4 › Activity 1*

UNIT OBJECTIVE

Read a product review and a news article. Gather information and ideas to write an essay comparing and contrasting two new technologies that can improve lives.

READING 1

Five Innovative Technologies That Bring Energy to the Developing World

OBJECTIVE ▶

You are going to read a product review by Joseph Stromberg for Smithsonian.com. The review looks at innovative energy technologies. Use the review to gather information and ideas for your Unit Assignment.

PREVIEW THE READING

A. PREVIEW Read the title. Read the headings and look at the pictures.

1. Try to guess what the five technologies are from their names and pictures.

2. Which of the five technologies seems most interesting? Why?

B. QUICK WRITE Imagine your life without electricity. How would it be different than your life with electricity? Compare the two. Write for 5–10 minutes in response. Remember to use this section for your Unit Assignment.

C. VOCABULARY Check (✓) the words you know. Use a dictionary to define any new or unknown words. Then discuss with a partner how the words will relate to the unit.

alleviate *(v.)*	grid *(n.)* 🔑+
dedicated *(adj.)* 🔑+	innovative *(adj.)* 🔑+
developing *(adj.)*	intuitively *(adv.)*
enterprise *(n.)* 🔑+	motion *(n.)* 🔑+
existence *(n.)* 🔑+ OPAL	replacement *(n.)* 🔑+ OPAL
generate *(v.)* 🔑+ OPAL	resemble *(v.)* 🔑+

🔑+ Oxford 5000™ words   **OPAL** Oxford Phrasal Academic Lexicon

iQ PRACTICE   Go online to listen and practice your pronunciation.
Practice ⟩ Unit 4 ⟩ Activity 2

WORK WITH THE READING

 A. INVESTIGATE Read the review and gather information about innovative energy technologies.

FIVE INNOVATIVE TECHNOLOGIES THAT BRING ENERGY TO THE DEVELOPING WORLD

By Joseph Stromberg

1   In the wealthy world, improving the energy system generally means increasing the central supply of reliable, inexpensive, and environmentally-friendly power. This power is then distributed through the power **grid**. Across most of the planet, though, millions of people are without electricity and depend on burning wood or kerosene[1] for heat and light. Simply providing new energy sources would open up new opportunities for these people and for engineers and designers.

2   With that in mind, engineers and designers have recently created a range of **innovative** devices that can increase the supply of safe, cheap energy on a user-by-user basis. The devices do not need the years it takes to extend the power grid to remote places. They also make it easier for countries to produce more energy without spending a lot more money. Here are a few of the most promising technologies.

VOTO

👍 Like   💬 Comment

3   Millions of people around the world use charcoal[2] and wood-fueled stoves on a daily basis. VOTO, developed by the company Point Source Power, converts the energy these fires release as heat into electricity. That electricity can power a handheld light, charge a phone, or even charge a spare battery. The company initially designed VOTO for backpackers and campers in wealthy countries, so they can charge their devices during trips. Now it is also trying to find a way for residents of the **developing** world to use it every day.

VOTO

The Window Socket

👍 Like   💬 Comment

4   This is perhaps the simplest solar charger in **existence**. Just stick it on a sunny window for 5–8 hours, with the built-in suction cup[3]. The solar panels on the back will store about ten hours' worth of electricity that can be used with any device. If there's no window available, a user can just leave it on any sunny surface, including the ground. Once it's fully charged, it can be removed and taken anywhere. It can be stored in a bag or carried around in a vehicle. The designers, Kyuho Song and Boa Oh of Yanko Design, created it to **resemble** a normal wall outlet[4] as closely as possible. In that way, it can be used **intuitively** without any special instructions.

The Window Socket

[1] **kerosene:** a type of fuel oil made of petroleum and that is used for heat and light
[2] **charcoal:** a black substance made by burning wood slowly in an oven with little air; used as a fuel
[3] **suction cup:** a cup-shaped device that produces a partial vacuum that makes it stick to a surface
[4] **wall outlet:** a device in a wall that you plug into to connect electrical equipment

The Berkeley-Darfur Stove

👍 Like 💬 Comment

5   In the past few years, a number of health researchers have come to the same conclusion: Providing a safe, energy-efficient, wood-burning cookstove to millions of people in the developing world has three major benefits. This kind of cookstove can directly improve health by reducing smoke inhalation[5]. It can aid the environment by reducing the amount of wood needed for fuel. It can **alleviate** poverty by reducing the amount of time needed to devote to gathering wood every day.

The Berkeley-Darfur Stove

6   Many projects have pursued this goal. Potential Energy, a nonprofit **dedicated** to adapting technologies to help improve lives in the developing world, is the furthest along. Potential Energy has distributed more than 25,000 of their Berkeley-Darfur Stoves in Darfur and Ethiopia. Their stove's design achieves these aims with features such as a wind collar that keeps the fire from burning too fast and air vents that reduce the amount of wind allowed to affect the fire, which decreases the amount of fuel wasted. It also has ridges that let the cook pot be at the best distance from the fire in order to use the fuel in the most efficient manner.

The GravityLight

👍 Like 💬 Comment

7   Kerosene-burning lamps provide light throughout the developing world. However, these lamps are targets for **replacement** because the fumes[6] **generated** by burning kerosene in close quarters are a major health problem. A seemingly simple solution is GravityLight, developed by deciwatt.org.

The GravityLight

8   To power the device, a user fills an included bag with about 20 pounds of rock or dirt. He or she attaches it to the cord hanging down from the device and lifts it upward. The potential energy stored in that lifting **motion** is then gradually converted to electricity by the GravityLight. It slowly lets the bag downward over the course of about 30 minutes and powers a light or other electrical device during that time. It's currently priced at about $10. Because it requires no cost to run, the development team estimates that the cost to buy it will be paid back in about three months by saving the money used to buy kerosene.

SOCCKET

👍 Like 💬 Comment

9   Soccer is easily the most popular sport in the world. The newest product of Uncharted Power, a for-profit social **enterprise**, seeks to take advantage of the millions of people already playing the sport. Uncharted Power wants to replace kerosene lamps with electric light that is generated in a much different manner. Their ball uses an internal motion-powered device to generate and store electricity. After about 30 minutes of play, the ball stores enough energy to power an attachable LED lamp for 3 hours. A percentage of all retail sales will go to providing SOCCKETs to schools in the developing world.

SOCCKET

[5] **inhalation:** the taking in of air, smoke, gas, etc., into the lungs as you breathe
[6] **fumes:** smoke, gas, or something similar that smells or is dangerous to breathe in

B. VOCABULARY Here are some words and phrases from Reading 1. Read the sentences. Circle the answer that best matches the meaning of each bold word.

VOCABULARY SKILL REVIEW

In Unit 3, you learned about prefixes that change a word's meaning and suffixes that change the part of speech. As you learn new words, find out whether you can apply these prefixes or suffixes to make related words.

1. Being connected to the power **grid** is a luxury. But we seldom think about the ____ until something disrupts it.

   a. network   b. plan   c. power

2. In our rapidly changing world, we depend on **innovative** solutions to the problems we face. We need ____ ideas and ways of doing things.

   a. big   b. new   c. smart

3. Providing technology to help people is the goal of most **developing** nations. These ____ societies, like wealthy societies, are trying to improve lives.

   a. rich   b. advanced   c. poor

4. This is the best technology in **existence** today. The technology is ____.

   a. not available yet   b. real and available   c. no longer available

5. Both daughters **resemble** their mother. They ____ her.

   a. like   b. look like   c. differ from

6. They didn't read the instructions. Rather, they still succeeded in using the device **intuitively**. They understood how to do it ____.

   a. well   b. quickly   c. without help

7. The ceiling fans **alleviated** our discomfort. Our problems were ____.

   a. made less severe   b. worsened   c. unaffected

8. They are **dedicated** to helping as many people as possible. They are ____ to achieving their goal because the work is important.

   a. committed   b. on their way   c. unwilling

9. We need a **replacement** for this policy, which is having a negative impact on the environment. We must provide ____.

   a. a place with clean air   b. a new reason   c. something better

10. Electricity can be **generated** by using wind. It can also be ____ by using the sun and water, for example.

    a. produced   b. consumed   c. wasted

11. **Motion** is necessary for good health. The ____ keeps us fit.

    a. ability to move   b. need for movement   c. process of moving

12. Much of the innovation in technology is the result of the efforts of an individual or small **enterprise**. Innovation seems to happen less often in a large ____.

a. industry

b. company

c. government organization

iQ PRACTICE   Go online for more practice with vocabulary. *Practice > Unit 4 > Activity 3*

C. **EXPLAIN** Discuss the questions with a partner.

1. What is the purpose of the review?

2. What are the advantages of all five of these technologies?

3. Who are the targeted users of these technologies?

4. Which technology uses solar power?

5. Which technology utilizes heat to provide electricity?

6. How does the GravityLight power a light?

 CRITICAL THINKING STRATEGY

Categorizing information

When you **categorize information**, you put it into groups by type. This can help you see the relationships between ideas more clearly. For example:

What the device produces or conserves		
Electricity		**Heat**
VOTO	Window Socket	Berkeley-Darfur Stove
GravityLight	SOCCKET	

iQ PRACTICE   Go online to watch the Critical Thinking Skill Video and check your comprehension. *Practice > Unit 4 > Activity 4*

D. CATEGORIZE Reread the descriptions of each technology in Reading 1. Then use the information to complete the charts.

What the electricity is used for	
Recharging devices	Producing light

What the device replaces		
Non-portable chargers	Less efficient stoves	Kerosene lamps

E. CATEGORIZE Read the statements. Write *T* (true) or *F* (false) and the paragraph number where the answer is found. Then correct each false statement to make it true according to the review.

____ 1. Few people today live off the power grid. (paragraph ____)

____ 2. Providing energy sources can open up new opportunities in developing countries. (paragraph ____)

____ 3. The VOTO converts the energy of wood-fueled stoves into energy to power lights, etc. (paragraph ____)

____ 4. The Window Socket uses solar panels to store ten hours of electricity. (paragraph ____)

____ 5. The Berkeley-Darfur Stove reduces the amount of wood needed for fuel. (paragraph ____)

____ 6. The GravityLight, designed to replace kerosene-burning lights, is expensive to buy. (paragraph ____)

____ 7. It costs a lot to use the GravityLight. (paragraph ____)

____ 8. Uncharted Power's SOCCKET is a solar energy light designed to replace kerosene lamps. (paragraph ____)

F. SYNTHESIZE Look back at your Quick Write on page 94. How would your life be without electricity? Add any new ideas or information you learned from the reading.

iQ PRACTICE Go online for additional reading and comprehension.
Practice > Unit 4 > Activity 5

WRITE WHAT YOU THINK

A. DISCUSS Discuss the questions in a group. Think about the Unit Question, "How can science improve lives?"

1. Which of the five technologies seems most practical? Least practical?

2. Which of the five technologies seems easiest to provide to people in areas that don't have access to electricity?

3. How can access to energy open up opportunities to people in developing nations? Give specific examples.

B. SYNTHESIZE Choose one of the questions from Activity A and write a paragraph of 5–7 sentences in response. Look back at your Quick Write on page 94 as you think about what you learned.

READING SKILL Understanding comparisons and contrasts

Writers **compare and contrast** information in order to examine the similarities and differences between two or more things. Phrases that signal similarities include *all (of), both, each, similarly, like,* and *likewise*. Phrases such as *in comparison with, by comparison, in contrast,* and *differs from* show differences. Comparisons can also be made using comparative and superlative adjectives: *better/worse, more/less . . . than, the best/worst*. Look at this paragraph:

> Five innovative technologies seek to improve lives in developing countries with quick, efficient energy sources. There are similarities and differences in how each of the five technologies provides energy. **All of** the technologies seek to provide safe sources of energy on a user-by-user basis. **Likewise,** each technology is designed to provide energy as cheaply as possible. The technologies **differ** in how they provide energy. Two use wood-burning stoves. The VOTO converts heat from existing wood-burning stoves into electricity to power various devices. **By comparison,** the Berkeley-Darfur Stove is a **better** wood-burning stove that is **more** efficient. The other three technologies seek to provide electricity in **less** harmful ways by harnessing existing clean energy sources. The Window Socket uses solar energy to provide electricity. **In contrast,** the GravityLight and the SOCCKET are designed to generate power using motion.

When a reading doesn't explicitly make comparisons, as is the case with Reading 1, it is up to the reader to understand and infer the similarities and differences using the information provided. You can use a simple T-chart to quickly identify and separate the information.

	Application of technology
Utilizes charcoal-/wood-fueled stoves	Harnesses existing clean energy sources to create electricity
The **VOTO** converts heat from wood-fueled stoves into electricity.	The **Window Socket** provides electricity using solar power.
The **Berkeley-Darfur Stove** provides a better wood-fueled stove that creates energy more efficiently.	The **GravityLight** replaces kerosene-burning lights with an electricity-generated light using gravity.
	The **SOCCKET** replaces kerosene-burning lights with an electric one using an internal motion-powered device.

You can also divide the information further by adding categories or topic areas down the side of the chart. After you chart the information, you can easily examine the ideas for similarities and differences.

A. CATEGORIZE Reread paragraphs 3–9 of Reading 1. Underline the phrases that describe each technology. Then write the information in the chart.

Device	Materials	Manner	Source of energy
VOTO	Charcoal-/wood-burning stove + VOTO device		
Window Socket		Solar panels store energy to use with any device (simple charger)	
Berkeley-Darfur Stove			Fire/Heat
GravityLight			
SOCCKET			

B. DISCUSS Discuss your chart with a partner and add any points that you missed. What similarities and differences do you see in the points?

iQ PRACTICE   Go online for more practice with understanding comparisons and contrasts. *Practice > Unit 4 > Activity 6*

This Device Pulls Water Out of Desert Air

OBJECTIVE ▶

You are going to read a news article by reporter Emily Matchar for Smithsonian.com. The article takes a look at a device that helps people live in arid places. Use the article to gather information and ideas for your Unit Assignment.

PREVIEW THE READING

A. PREVIEW Look at the title and subtitle. Why would a device like this be useful? Read the last paragraph. What do you think "water-stressed regions" are? How much water "satisfies the basic needs of the individuals"?

B. QUICK WRITE The average person needs about 10 gallons (38 liters) of clean water a day for drinking and cleaning. Imagine you had only 2 gallons (7.5 liters). What would you have to give up or do differently? Write for 5–10 minutes in response. Remember to use this section for your Unit Assignment.

C. VOCABULARY Check (✓) the words you know. Use a dictionary to define any new or unknown words. Then discuss with a partner how the words will relate to the unit.

absorb *(v.)* 🔊+	organic *(adj.)* 🔊+
caution *(v.)* 🔊+	porous *(adj.)*
drought *(n.)* 🔊+	potentially *(adv.)* 🔊+ OPAL
extract *(v.)* 🔊+	premise *(n.)* 🔊+
framework *(n.)* 🔊+ OPAL	shortage *(n.)* 🔊+
implication *(n.)* 🔊+	yield *(n.)* 🔊+ OPAL

🔊+ Oxford 5000™ words   **OPAL** Oxford Phrasal Academic Lexicon

iQ PRACTICE Go online to listen and practice your pronunciation.
Practice > Unit 4 > Activity 7

WORK WITH THE READING

 A. INVESTIGATE Read the article and gather information about a device that helps people live in arid places.

THIS DEVICE PULLS WATER OUT OF DESERT AIR

A water harvester based on MOF technology

A new water harvester[1] can extract water from extremely dry air using only solar energy.

By Emily Matchar

1 **Droughts** have been making headlines across the world in recent years, from the California water crisis to Cape Town's severe water **shortage**. Research suggests 25 percent of the globe could eventually be left in permanent drought due to climate change. But what if you could simply pull water from the air?

2 That's the **premise** of a new technology developed by University of California, Berkeley researchers. It's a water harvester that can **extract** water from the air, even in extremely dry climates. It uses no energy other than ambient[2] sunlight.

3 The key to the water harvester is a new class of materials called *metal-**organic frameworks*** (MOFs). These MOFs are solid but **porous**

materials with enormous surface areas. An MOF the size of a sugar cube can have the internal surface area as big as many football fields. This means that they can **absorb** gases and liquids, and then release them quickly when heat is added.

4 "Certain MOFs have an extraordinary ability to suck in water vapor from the atmosphere, but then at the same time do not hold on to the water molecules inside their pores too tightly so that it is easy to get the water out," says Omar Yaghi. He is a professor of chemistry at Berkeley and led the research.

5 The researchers tested the harvester in Scottsdale, Arizona. It is a desert town with a high of 40 percent humidity at night

---

[1] **water harvester:** a machine that gathers water
[2] **ambient:** relating to the surrounding area; on all sides

and 8 percent humidity during the day. The researchers believe that the harvester could ultimately extract about 3 ounces of water per pound of MOF per day.

6   The harvester itself is a box inside a box. The inner box contains a bed of MOFs. The outer box is a two-foot transparent[3] plastic cube. At night, the researchers left the top off the outer box to let air flow past the MOFs. In the day, they put the top back on, so the box would be heated by the sun. The heat would pull the water out of the MOFs, where it would condense on the inner walls of the plastic cube before dripping to the bottom, where it could be collected.

7   "The most important aspect of this technology is that it is completely energy-passive," says Eugene Kapustin, a Berkeley graduate student who worked on the research. That is to say, it needs no energy besides the sun. This makes it environmentally friendly and accessible[4] to people in places with limited electricity. The results of the trials were published in the journal *Science Advances* (Fathieh, 2018).

8   The team needs to conduct more trials on the current models to figure out which factors most affect how much water can be harvested. They also hope to learn more about how specific climate conditions affect water **yield**. The next trial is planned for late summer in Death Valley, where the nighttime humidity can be as low as 25 percent.

9   Yaghi has also developed a new aluminum-based MOF. He says it is 150 times cheaper and can capture twice as much water as the current MOFs. He and his team are designing a new water harvester that actively pulls air into the MOFs at high speed. It thus delivers a much larger volume of water.

10   The team is now partnering with industry to test harvesters on an industrial scale. They also continue to search for newer, better, and cheaper MOFs. "I am very happy to see that more and more researchers around the world are joining our efforts in this regard," Yaghi says.

11   The idea of sucking water out of the atmosphere is not new, says Eric Hoek. He is an engineering professor at the University of California, Los Angeles and editor of the journal *npj Clean Water*. It's long been noted that when you run an air conditioner, water drips out. This is because the machine is cooling the air to the dew point, the temperature at which the air is saturated with water vapor and condensation occurs.

12   But creating water harvesters based on cooling technology is incredibly energy intense. In very dry climates, the dew point is below zero. Cooling the air to that temperature at any large scale is unfeasible.

13   "The real innovation [of Yaghi's research] is a materials innovation," Hoek says. "These materials [the MOFs] pull water out and more easily give it up." But the concept is challenging to scale[5], Hoek **cautions**, as the amount of water produced per square inch of harvester is relatively low. Thus a large harvester would **potentially** take up a huge amount of land. "But maybe for a household or village, it could be a very interesting way for someone to get fresh water," Hoek says.

14   Yaghi imagines exactly that: a future where everyone without easy access to fresh water has a harvester in their yard.

15   "My vision is to achieve 'personalized water,' where people in water-stressed regions have a device at home running on ambient solar, delivering the water that satisfies the basic needs of the individuals," he says. "More than one third of the population in the world lives in water-stressed regions or is suffering from a lack of clean water. The potential **implications** of this technology in transforming people's lives and improving the global public health conditions are tremendous."

Reference Fathieh, Farhad et al. (2018). Practical Water Production from Air. *Science Advances, 4* (6)

[3] **transparent:** something that can be seen through
[4] **accessible:** something that can be reached, entered, used, seen, etc.
[5] **scale:** to change the size of something

B. VOCABULARY Here are some words from Reading 2. Read the sentences. Then write each bold word next to the correct definition. You may need to change verbs to their base form and nouns to the singular form.

1. The **premise** that drives their research is the idea that many people need access to clean water.

2. The **implication** of the research is that, with this technology, it is possible to ensure an adequate supply of water.

3. The device uses a simple **framework** of two boxes, one inside the other.

4. **Organic** materials always contain some carbon since carbon is a basic element of living things.

5. Long **droughts** often lead to wildfires because plants dry up and burn easily.

6. If we have a **shortage** of water, we may need to give up taking long showers.

7. The purpose of a paper towel is to **absorb** water or other liquids.

8. We put sand in the soil to make the soil more **porous**, letting water move through it more easily.

9. The professor **cautioned** us to not spend too much time on our project.

10. We wanted to **extract** the salt from the sea water so that we could drink the water.

11. There are **potentially** many uses for this device; the possibilities are many.

12. Farmers need to estimate the **yield** for each field, so they can estimate how much money they will make.

a. _____ (n.) a possible effect or result of an action or a decision

b. _____ (n.) the parts of an object that support its weight and give it shape

c. _____ (n.) a statement or an idea that forms the basis of an argument

d. _____ (v.) to take in a liquid, gas, or other substance from the surface or space around

e. _____ (n.) a situation when there is not enough of the people or things that are needed

f. _____ (adj.) having many small holes that allow water or air to pass through slowly

g. _____ (v.) to remove or obtain a substance from something

h. _____ (n.) a long period of time when there is little or no rain

i. _____ (v.) to warn somebody about the possible dangers or problems of something

j. _____ (n.) the total amount of crops, profits, etc., that are produced

k. _____ (adv.) used to say that something may happen; possibly

l. _____ (adj) produced by or from living things

iQ PRACTICE Go online for more practice with the vocabulary.
Practice > Unit 4 > Activity 8

C. IDENTIFY Circle the correct answer. Then write the paragraph number where the answer is found.

1. What are MOFs (metal-organic frameworks)? (paragraph ____)
   a. solid materials that are small but have a lot of surface area
   b. materials that take in liquids and gases
   c. materials that release liquids and gases when they are heated
   d. all of the above

2. A water harvester is a box inside a box. What is the purpose of the outside box? (paragraph ____)
   a. It protects the inside box from animals.
   b. It collects the water that evaporates.
   c. It makes the water harvester easier to see.
   d. It focuses the sunlight on the box.

3. Why is the lid taken off the water harvester at night? (paragraph ____)
   a. to make it easier to inspect
   b. to allow the MOFs to absorb water
   c. to dry the MOFs
   d. to let insects drink the water from the box

4. Why is the lid put on the water harvester during the day? (paragraph ____)

    a. so that the MOF can absorb sunlight

    b. so that it can reflect the heat away from the box

    c. so that the box will trap the water released by the MOF

    d. so that dirt and animals don't get into the box

5. What is the main problem with water harvesters? (paragraph ____)

    a. They don't yield much water for their size.

    b. They use a lot of energy.

    c. They are hard to maintain.

    d. They weigh too much.

D. RESTATE Write the meaning of these phrases from the article.

1. energy-passive (paragraph 7) _____

2. conduct more trials (paragraph 8) _____

3. nighttime humidity (paragraph 8) _____

4. sucking water out of the atmosphere (paragraph 11)

_____

5. dew point (paragraphs 11 and 12) _____

6. "personalized water" (paragraph 15) _____

E. EXPLAIN Discuss the questions with a partner.

1. What is the major benefit of the water harvesters?

2. Why do the scientists test the water harvesters in deserts?

3. What are two benefits of the water harvesters being "energy-passive"?

4. Why would Omar Yaghi "test harvesters on an industrial scale" (paragraph 10)?

5. Why don't scientists cool the air to get the water out of it?

6. Reread the last sentence in the article. How could a water harvester transform someone's life?

WORK WITH THE VIDEO

A. PREVIEW Can we do something about global warming? If so, what?

VIDEO VOCABULARY

reflective (adj.) sending back heat or light

enhance (v.) to increase or further improve the good quality of something

particle (n.) a very small piece of something

vapor (n.) a mass of very small drops of liquid in the air

replicating (n.) producing exact copies of

iQ RESOURCES Go online to watch the video about geoengineering inventions used to save the planet by combatting global warming.
Resources > Video > Unit 4 > Unit Video

B. COMPOSE Watch the video two or three times. Take notes in the chart.

	Putting tiny reflective lenses into space	Making clouds thicker and more reflective	Releasing sulfur into the stratosphere
Notes from the video			
My ideas			

C. EXTEND What are the advantages and disadvantages of each invention? Which idea seems the most likely to work? Write your ideas in the chart above. Discuss your ideas with a partner.

WRITE WHAT YOU THINK

SYNTHESIZE Think about Reading 1, Reading 2, and the unit video as you discuss these questions. Then choose one question and write a paragraph of 5–7 sentences in response.

1. Some inventions start out being for one group of people but end up being useful for other groups of people as well, such as the VOTO in Reading 1. Which of the technologies in the readings and the video could you use?

2. Many technologies have both positive and negative aspects. Choose a technology that you use (cell phone, automobile, etc.). What are the positive and negative points of that technology?

3. A popular expression in English is, "Necessity is the mother of invention." Think of a need you know of in any country, in any field. What technology, existing or imagined, would address that need?

VOCABULARY SKILL Using the dictionary to distinguish between homonyms

---

Finding the correct meaning

There are many words that have the same spelling and pronunciation but different meanings. These words are called *homonyms*.

> **lift** *(v.)* to raise something to a higher position
>> I **lifted** the lid of the box and peered in.
>
> **lift** *(v.)* to copy ideas or words without asking permission
>> She **lifted** most of the ideas from a book she had been reading.
>
> **lift** *(v.)* to become or make more cheerful
>> His heart **lifted** at the sight of a house in the distance.
>
> **field** *(n.)* (usually in compounds) an area of land used for the purpose mentioned
>> Her excitement grew as she kicked the ball down the soccer **field**.
>
> **field** *(n.)* a particular subject or activity that somebody works in or is interested in
>> He is an expert in the **field** of chemistry.

Some homonyms may have different parts of speech, for example, a noun form and a verb form.

> **scale** *(n.)* the size of something
>> The team is now testing harvesters on an industrial **scale**.
>
> **scale** *(v.)* to change the size of something
>> The concept is challenging to **scale**.

Advanced dictionaries will list all the word forms and definitions for them. When using a dictionary to find the correct meaning of a word, it is important to read the entire sentence where you found the word and consider the use and context.

A. IDENTIFY Look at the dictionary entry for *range*. Check (✓) the correct answers.

range 🔊 ⓞ /reɪndʒ/ *noun, verb*
- *noun*
> **VARIETY 1** [C, usually sing.] ~ **(of sth)** a variety of things of a particular type: *The hotel offers a **wide range** of facilities.* ♦ *There is **a full range of** activities for kids.*
> **LIMITS 2** [C, usually sing.] the limits between which something varies: *Most of the students are in the 17–20 **age range**.* ♦ *There will be an increase **in the range** of 0 to 3 percent.* ♦ *It's difficult to find a house in our **price range** (= that we can afford).* ♦ *This was **outside the range of his experience**.*
> **DISTANCE 3** [C, U] the distance over which something can be seen or heard: *The child was now out of her **range of vision** (= not near enough for her to see).* **4** [C, U] the distance over which a gun or other weapon can hit things: *These missiles have a range of 300 miles.* **5** [C] the distance that a vehicle will travel before it needs more fuel
> **MUSIC 6** [C, usually sing.] all of the notes that a person's voice or a musical instrument can produce, from high to low: *She was gifted with an incredible vocal range.*
> **ABILITY 7** [C, usually sing.] the full extent of a person's knowledge or abilities: *Those two movies give some indication of his range as an actor.*
> **OF MOUNTAINS 8** [C] a line or group of mountains or hills: *the great mountain range of the Alps*
> **FOR SHOOTING 9** [C] an area of land where people can practice shooting or where bombs, etc. can be tested: *a shooting range*
> **OF PRODUCTS 10** [C] a set of products of a particular type `SYN` **LINE:** *our new range of hair products*
- *verb*
> **VARY 1** [I] to vary between two particular amounts, sizes, etc., including others between them: ~ **from A to B** *to range in size/length/price from A to B* ♦ *Accommodations range from tourist class to luxury hotels.* ♦ ~ **between A and B** *Estimates of the damage range between $1 million and $5 million.* **2** [I] to include a variety of different things in addition to those mentioned: ~ **from A to B** *She has had a number of different jobs, ranging from chef to swimming instructor.* ♦ **+ adv./prep.** *The conversation ranged widely (= covered a lot of different topics).*
> **ARRANGE 3** [T, usually passive] ~ **sb/sth/yourself + adv./prep.** (*formal*) to arrange people or things in a particular position or order: *The delegates ranged themselves around the table.* ♦ *Spectators were ranged along the whole route of the procession.*
> **MOVE AROUND 4** [I, T] to move around an area: **+ adv./prep.** *He ranges far and wide in search of inspiration for his paintings.* ♦ ~ **sth** *Her eyes ranged the room.*

All dictionary entries adapted from the *Oxford American Dictionary for learners of English* © Oxford University Press 2011.

1. *Range* can be used as:

☐ a noun   ☐ an adjective

☐ a verb   ☐ an adverb

2. *Range* can mean:

☐ to vary   ☐ light

☐ distance over which something can be heard or seen   ☐ to move around

                                          ☐ music

☐ to lift

B. IDENTIFY Read the excerpts from Readings 1 and 2. Look up each bold word in your dictionary. Write the part of speech and the correct definition based on the context.

Reading 1

1. The devices do not need the years it takes to extend the **power** grid to remote places.

   _____

2. That electricity can power a handheld light, **charge** a phone, or even charge a spare battery.

   _____

3. Just **stick** it on a sunny window for 5–8 hours, with the built-in suction cup.

   _____

4. The solar panels on the back will **store** about ten hours' worth of electricity that can be used with any device.

   _____

5. With that in mind, engineers and designers have recently created a range of innovative devices that can increase the supply of **safe**, cheap energy on a user-by-user basis.

   _____

Reading 2

6. In the day, they put the top back on, so the box would be **heated** by the sun.

   _____

7. The heat would pull the water out of the MOFs, where it would **condense** on the inner walls of the plastic cube before dripping to the bottom, where it could be collected.

   _____

8. Cooling the air to that temperature at any large **scale** is unfeasible.

   _____

iQ PRACTICE Go online for more practice with using the dictionary to distinguish between homonyms. _Practice > Unit 4 > Activity 9_

WRITING

OBJECTIVE ▶

At the end of this unit, you will write an essay comparing and contrasting two new technologies that can improve lives. This essay will include specific information from the readings, the unit video, and your own ideas.

WRITING SKILL Writing a compare and contrast essay

A **compare and contrast essay** describes the similarities and differences between two subjects. Comparisons show their similarities, while contrasts examine their differences.

Introduction

The introduction describes the two subjects being compared and contrasted. It has a thesis statement that explains the relationship between the two subjects or gives reasons why the relationship is important.

Body paragraphs

There are many different ways to organize the body paragraphs of a compare and contrast essay. Before you write a compare and contrast essay, it is important to decide which organization is best for your essay. Here are two ways to organize your ideas:

- In a **point by point essay**, you choose three or more key points to compare and contrast. Each body paragraph compares and contrasts one key point. This organization can be best when you want to balance your essay evenly between your two subjects.

- In a **similarities and differences essay**, the first body paragraph explains what is similar about the two subjects. The second body paragraph explains what is different about the two subjects. The third body paragraph discusses the most important similarities and differences. This organization can be best when you want to explain why one subject is better than the other subject, or what is significant about their similarities or differences.

Conclusion

The conclusion summarizes the similarities and differences and gives the writer's opinion about the topic. It can explain why one of the subjects is better than the other or why they are of equal value.

iQ RESOURCES Go online to watch the Writing Skill Video.
Resources > Video > Unit 4 > Writing Skill Video

A. WRITING MODEL Read the model compare and contrast essay. Then answer the questions that follow.

The Dream of Flight

Otto Lilienthal

The Wright brothers

1.   Flying has long been a dream of many people. Two sets of brothers are universally acknowledged to have contributed immensely to heavier-than-air flight. These brothers, the Lilienthals of Germany and the Wrights of the United States, share some similarities but also have some differences.

2.   The Lilienthals, Otto and Gustav, worked together, as did the Wrights, Orville and Wilbur. Unlike the Wright brothers, who are usually spoken of together, the Lillienthal brothers weren't equally famous. Otto is usually spoken of individually. Otto opened a business that made boilers and steam engines, which made enough money for him to pursue his hobby of flight. When engaging with aircraft, Otto always worked with Gustav. The Wright brothers opened a printing business and then a bicycle shop. They developed their innovations to the airplane together as well. They shared credit for their inventions and depended on their businesses, including their work in aviation, to make a living.

3.   While Otto Lilienthal was educated and employed as an engineer, the Wright brothers did not study at a university. The Wright brothers were mostly self-taught. In fact, one of the books that the Wrights were inspired by was authored by Otto Lilienthal.

4.   Both Otto Lilienthal and the Wright brothers were inventors; many of their patents were related to aircraft. Otto and the Wright brothers were interested in gliders, specifically in how to control them. Both Otto Lilienthal and the Wrights studied birds in order to ascertain how birds were able to control themselves in flight. Otto, who made over 2,000 flights in gliders, was known as "the father of flight" because he was the first to sustain a controlled flight in a heavier-than-air aircraft, a glider. The Wrights are credited with the three-axis control (up and down, side to side, and forward and backward) for aircraft, which is still used in fixed-wing aircraft today. They are also credited with achieving the first sustained, controlled flight of an airplane. The Lilienthals and the Wrights were both influential in developing heavier-than-air aircraft, especially contributing to the control of the aircraft. Otto Lilienthal held patents on his inventions. Similarly, the Wright brothers held patents on their inventions and went on to build airplanes.

5.   Despite their differences, the Lilienthals and the Wright brothers will always be remembered for their contributions to helping people achieve the dream of flight.

1. What is the thesis statement? Underline it.

2. How is the essay organized? _____

3. Why do you think the author organized it this way?

_____

B. CATEGORIZE Reread the essay on page 113. Complete the chart with both the similarities and the differences for each key point. Then compare with a partner.

Compare and contrast essay: Point by point		
Key points	**The Lilienthal brothers**	**The Wright brothers**
1. supporting businesses		
2. education		
3. inventions/interest in flight		

C. CATEGORIZE Work with a partner. Complete the chart below. Reorganize the information from the essay into a plan for a similarities and differences essay. Use the chart in Activity B to help you.

Compare and contrast essay: Similarities and differences		
Similarities	**Differences**	
	The Lilienthal brothers	**The Wright brothers**

D. CATEGORIZE Use the chart to help you think of examples of technology 100 years ago and technology now.

Compare and contrast essay: Similarities and differences		
Similarities	**Differences**	
	Technology 100 years ago	**Technology now**

E. WRITING MODEL Read the model compare and contrast essay. Then answer the questions that follow.

Two Chemicals That Have Changed Lives

1   How has chemistry improved your life? When not one chemist made the top 50 scientists in *Science* magazine in 2014, the Royal Academy of Chemistry decided to try to understand why. It seems that when we think of innovations, chemistry is often overlooked. But, in fact, chemistry has led to many improvements in our lives. Two other important innovations in chemistry, penicillin and ammonia, have contributed to the world as we know it today, though each has done so in different ways.

2   Both penicillin and ammonia are naturally occurring on earth. Penicillin is a mold, and ammonia is a chemical compound. They were also both discovered around the same time. Penicillin was discovered in 1928, by Scottish bacteriologist Alexander Fleming. Just more than a decade later, Australian pharmacologist Howard Florey purified penicillin into useable amounts, and in 1944, chemical engineer Margaret Hutchinson Rousseau was able to put it into production. Similarly, in 1910, German chemists Fritz Haber and Carl Bosch were working on the formulation that would become ammonia. They did it by combining nitrogen and hydrogen. This process of making ammonia, called the *Haber-Bosch process*, allowed for the greater access to nitrogen of both plants and animals. Both penicillin and ammonia have been used to improve our lives.

3   While penicillin and ammonia share similarities, there are differences. The main difference is in how they are used. Penicillin is an important medical treatment used to cure many bacterial diseases. It has saved the lives of millions of people since it was first put into full-scale production in 1944. Ammonia, on the other hand, has been used mostly as a fertilizer, resulting in increased food production, cited as the most important factor in the population explosion over the last century.

4   However, the most significant similarity between these two innovations is how they are used and perceived today. With both, there is caution in their use. The reasons for that caution are very similar. Penicillin's use (or some would argue, overuse) has resulted in bacteria that are increasingly resistant to penicillin. Therefore, doctors are much more careful now in prescribing it to their patients. Similarly, ammonia is now understood to be a toxic chemical compound that is irritating and caustic. This has resulted in efforts to find alternatives to using it.

5   In conclusion, no one would dispute that these two chemistry inventions, penicillin and ammonia, have improved our lives since their discovery and development in the early twentieth century. But they have also shown us that even a good thing must be used carefully. Chemists must continue to conduct research on the chemicals that we use to improve lives.

1. What is the thesis statement? Underline it.

2. How is the essay organized?

_____

3. Why do you think the author organized it this way?

_____

F. CATEGORIZE Create a chart for the essay "Two Chemicals That Have Changed Lives" like the ones in Activities C and D.

iQ PRACTICE Go online for more practice writing a compare and contrast essay. *Practice > Unit 4 > Activity 10*

GRAMMAR Subordinators and transitions to compare and contrast

You can use different words and phrases to **compare and contrast** ideas.

Subordinators showing contrast

You can use an adverb clause to show an idea that contrasts with the main clause. The subordinators *although* and *though* show contrasting ideas. *Whereas* and *while* often signal more direct opposition. Notice the comma when the adverb clause comes first.

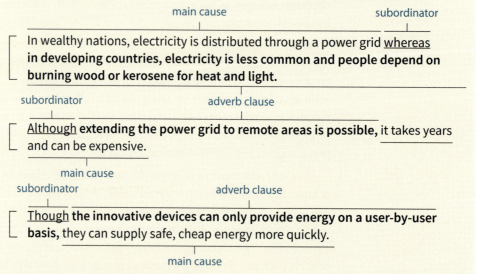

Transitions showing comparison

You can use some transition words to show comparison. Some common transition words to introduce comparison are *similarly, likewise,* and *in addition.* These are used to discuss similarities.

The GravityLight is a replacement for kerosene lamps. **Similarly**, the SOCCKET replaces kerosene lamps with an electric light.

All of the innovative devices provide energy on a user-by-user basis. **In addition,** they use sources that are readily available.

Providing new energy sources would open up new opportunities for people in developing countries. **Likewise,** it opens up opportunities for engineers and designers.

Transitions showing contrast

You can use other transition words to show contrast or differences.

Contrast	More direct opposition	Concession
however though	on the other hand in contrast	nevertheless in spite of this nonetheless despite this

Both the GravityLight and the SOCCKET replace kerosene lamps. **However,** they use different methods to generate electricity.

The GravityLight uses the energy generated by a falling motion to create electricity for the light. **On the other hand,** the SOCCKET uses an internal motion-powered device to generate and store electricity.

ACADEMIC LANGUAGE

The corpus shows that *in contrast* and *in contrast to* are often used in academic writing.
. . . In contrast, ammonia is . . .
. . . In contrast to penicillin, ammonia is . . .

⌐ OPAL
Oxford Phrasal Academic Lexicon

A. IDENTIFY Read each sentence. Underline the word or phrase that indicates a comparison or a contrast. Then write *CP* (comparison) or *CT* (contrast).

____ 1. The GravityLight and the SOCCKET each uses motion to generate energy, though they use different types of motion.

____ 2. The Berkeley-Darfur Stove helps users directly, improving health by reducing the amount of smoke inhaled. Similarly, it helps users by shortening the amount time spent gathering wood to fuel the stove.

____ 3. Each of the innovative technologies described in the review provides energy simply and safely. Nonetheless, some of them are more effective than others.

____ 4. While the Window Socket uses solar energy to generate power, VOTO uses the heat produced by a charcoal- or wood-burning stove.

____ 5. The electricity produced by VOTO can power a phone. Likewise, VOTO can even charge a spare battery.

B. IDENTIFY Circle the best phrase to complete each sentence.

1. The Wright brothers shared fame equally whereas *Otto Lilienthal was more famous than his brother, Gustav / the Lilienthal brothers were also equally famous*.

2. The Wright brothers had patents. Likewise, Otto Lilienthal *never had patents / had patents*.

3. Although the Wright brothers were self-educated, Otto Lilienthal *was also self-educated / was an engineer*.

4. The Wright brothers were self-educated. Despite this, they *built airplanes / didn't build airplanes*.

5. Otto Lilienthal is credited with the first heavier-than-air flight in a glider. In contrast, the Wright brothers *also are credited with heavier-than-air flight in a glider / are credited with heavier-than-air flight in an airplane*.

C. APPLY Complete the sentences using your own ideas. Make sure you use correct punctuation.

1. I think that science can improve lives. Nevertheless _____
   _____.

2. Although penicillin has saved many lives _____
   _____.

3. Water is essential to all living things. Similarly _____
   _____.

4. I think I could live without a television. On the other hand
   _____
   _____.

5. Technology has benefitted us in many ways. However
   _____
   _____.

6. Whereas many people in the world get electricity from a power grid
   _____
   _____.

iQ PRACTICE Go online for more practice with subordinators and transitions to compare and contrast. *Practice > Unit 4 > Activities 11–12*

Write a compare and contrast essay

In this assignment, you are going to write a five-paragraph essay comparing and contrasting two innovative technologies that can improve lives. As you prepare your essay, think about the Unit Question, "How can science improve lives?" Use information from Reading 1, Reading 2, the unit video, and your work in this unit to support your essay. Refer to the Self-Assessment checklist on page 120.

iQ PRACTICE   Go online to the Writing Tutor to read a model compare and contrast paragraph. *Practice › Unit 4 › Activity 13*

PLAN AND WRITE

WRITING TIP

When you brainstorm ideas using both a point by point and a similarities and differences chart, it will help you discover which organization works best for your subject, and you may get more ideas.

A. BRAINSTORM Follow these steps to help you organize your ideas.

1. Complete the chart. List new technologies that scientists have discovered, invented, or designed to improve lives in the fields indicated. Add another field and technologies you are familiar with. Compare charts with a partner.

Field	Technologies
Chemistry	
Physics	
Engineering	
Education	

2. Choose the two technologies you would like to use as your subject to compare and contrast.

3. Write points to compare and contrast and similarities and differences for your subject. (Refer to the charts on p. 114 to help you organize your ideas.)

B. PLAN Plan your essay.

Look at your ideas from question 3 in Activity A. Decide whether your essay would be best organized as a point by point essay or a similarities and differences essay.

iQ RESOURCES   Go online to download and complete the outline for your compare and contrast essay. *Resources › Writing Tools › Unit 4 › Outline*

C. WRITE Use your planning notes to write your essay.

1. Write your essay comparing and contrasting two innovative technologies to improve lives. Be sure to include an introduction with a thesis statement, three body paragraphs, and a conclusion.

2. Look at the Self-Assessment checklist on page 120 to guide your writing.

iQ PRACTICE   Go online to the Writing Tutor to write your assignment.
Practice > Unit 4 > Activity 14

REVISE AND EDIT

iQ RESOURCES   Go online to download the peer review worksheet.
Resources > Writing Tools > Unit 4 > Peer Review Worksheet

A. PEER REVIEW Read your partner's essay. Then use the peer review worksheet. Discuss the review with your partner.

B. REWRITE Based on your partner's review, revise and rewrite your essay.

C. EDIT Complete the Self-Assessment checklist as you prepare to write the final draft of your essay. Be prepared to hand in your work or discuss it in class.

SELF-ASSESSMENT	Yes	No
Does the thesis statement explain the relationship between the two subjects or give reasons why the relationship is important?	☐	☐
Is the essay organized using one of the compare and contrast essay types?	☐	☐
Does the essay contain an introduction, three body paragraphs, and a conclusion?	☐	☐
Does the essay use subordinators and transitions to compare and contrast?	☐	☐
Does the essay include vocabulary from the unit?	☐	☐
Did you check the essay for punctuation, spelling, and grammar?	☐	☐

D. REFLECT Discuss these questions with a partner or group.

1. What is something new you learned in this unit?

2. Look back at the Unit Question—How can science improve lives? Is your answer different now than when you started the unit? If yes, how is it different? Why?

iQ PRACTICE   Go to the online discussion board to discuss the questions.
Practice > Unit 4 > Activity 15

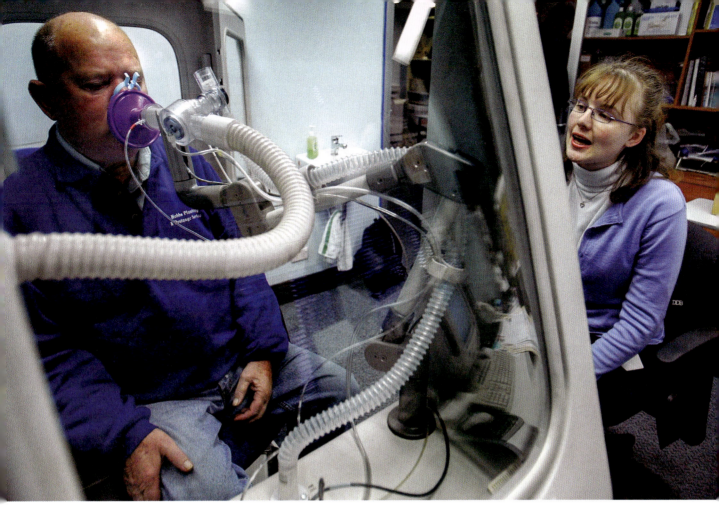

TRACK YOUR SUCCESS

iQ PRACTICE   Go online to check the words and phrases you have learned in this unit. *Practice > Unit 4 > Activity 16*

Check (✓) the skills and strategies you learned. If you need more work on a skill, refer to the page(s) in parentheses.

CRITICAL THINKING   ☐ I can categorize information. (p. 98)

READING   ☐ I can understand comparisons and contrasts. (p. 100)

VOCABULARY   ☐ I can use the dictionary to distinguish between homonyms. (p. 109)

WRITING   ☐ I can write a compare and contrast essay. (p. 112)

GRAMMAR   ☐ I can use subordinators and transitions to compare and contrast. (p. 116)

OBJECTIVE ▶   ☐ I can gather information and ideas to write an essay comparing and contrasting two new technologies that can improve lives.

ℝ+ The **Oxford 5000™** is an expanded core word list for advanced learners of English. The words have been chosen based on their frequency in the Oxford English Corpus and relevance to learners of English. As well as the Oxford 3000™ core word list, the Oxford 5000 includes an additional 2,000 words that are aligned to the CEFR, guiding advanced learners at B2-C1 level on the most useful high-level words to learn to expand their vocabulary.

OPAL The **Oxford Phrasal Academic Lexicon** is an essential guide to the most important words and phrases to know for academic English. The word lists are based on the Oxford Corpus of Academic English and the British Academic Spoken English corpus.

The **Common European Framework of Reference for Language (CEFR)** provides a basic description of what language learners have to do to use language effectively. The system contains 6 reference levels: A1, A2, B1, B2, C1, C2.

UNIT 1

achievement *(n.)* ℝ+ OPAL B1
acknowledged for *(adj. phr.)* B2
adversity *(n.)* C1
advocate *(n.)* ℝ+ C1
aspire to *(v. phr.)* ℝ+ C1
authenticity *(n.)* C1
cause *(n.)* ℝ+ OPAL A2
confront *(v.)* ℝ+ C1
constrained *(adj.)* OPAL C1
diverse *(adj.)* ℝ+ OPAL B2
embody *(v.)* ℝ+ OPAL C1
empower *(v.)* ℝ+ OPAL C1
exponential *(adj.)* C2
funding *(n.)* ℝ+ OPAL B2
humanitarian *(adj.)* ℝ+ C1
humility *(n.)* C2
inclined *(adj.)* ℝ+ C1
inherently *(adv.)* C1
perceive *(v.)* ℝ+ OPAL B2
personify *(v.)* C2
phenomenon *(n.)* ℝ+ OPAL B2
pursue *(adj.)* ℝ+ B2
resolve *(n.)* ℝ+ OPAL B2
version *(n.)* ℝ+ OPAL B1

UNIT 2

activation *(n.)* ℝ+ C1
align *(v.)* ℝ+ C1

allure *(n.)* C2
assume *(v.)* ℝ+ OPAL B2
broadly speaking *(adv. phr.)* B2
counter *(v.)* ℝ+ C1
crave *(v.)* C2
disclose *(v.)* ℝ+ C1
distinct *(adj.)* ℝ+ OPAL B2
endorse *(v.)* ℝ+ C1
escalate *(v.)* ℝ+ C1
essentially *(adv.)* ℝ+ OPAL B2
exaggerated *(adj.)* ℝ+ C1
functional *(adj.)* ℝ+ OPAL C1
impulsive *(adj.)* C1
insight *(n.)* ℝ+ OPAL B2
manipulate *(v.)* ℝ+ C1
metric *(n.)* C2
obsession *(n.)* ℝ+ C1
put a premium on *(v. phr.)* C2
resistance *(n.)* ℝ+ OPAL C1
tactic *(n.)* ℝ+ C1
tolerant *(adj.)* C1
transparency *(n.)* ℝ+ C1

UNIT 3

anxiety *(n.)* ℝ+ OPAL B2
attribute *(v.)* ℝ+ OPAL C1
barrier *(n.)* ℝ+ OPAL B2
coping *(n.)* ℝ+ B2

courage *(n.)* ℝ+ B2
empathy *(n.)* C1
encounter *(v.)* ℝ+ OPAL B2
extensive *(adj.)* ℝ+ OPAL B2
fit in *(v. phr.)* B2
foundation *(n.)* ℝ+ B2
hesitation *(n.)* C1
interaction *(n.)* ℝ+ OPAL B2
intervention *(n.)* ℝ+ OPAL C1
negotiate *(v.)* ℝ+ B2
petrified *(adj.)* C2
pitch in *(v. phr.)* C2
refrain *(n.)* C2
self-fulfillment *(n.)* C2
shame *(n.)* ℝ+ B2
tragic *(adj.)* ℝ+ B2
void *(n.)* C2
work ethic *(n. phr.)* C2
wounded *(adj.)* ℝ+ B2

UNIT 4

absorb *(v.)* ℝ+ B2
alleviate *(v.)* C1
caution *(v.)* ℝ+ C1
dedicated *(adj.)* ℝ+ C1
developing *(adj.)* B1
drought *(n.)* ℝ+ B2
enterprise *(n.)* ℝ+ C1
existence *(n.)* ℝ+ OPAL B2

extract *(v.)* + B2
framework *(n.)* + OPAL B2
generate *(v.)* + OPAL B2
grid *(n.)* + C1
implication *(n.)* + B2
innovative *(adj.)* + B2
intuitively *(adv.)* C1
motion *(n.)* + B2
organic *(adj.)* + B2
porous *(adj.)* C2
potentially *(adv.)* + OPAL B2
premise *(n.)* + C1
replacement *(n.)* + OPAL C1
resemble *(v.)* + C1
shortage *(n.)* + B2
yield *(n.)* + OPAL C1

UNIT 5

access *(n.)* + OPAL B1
approach *(n.)* + OPAL B2
benefit *(n.)* + OPAL A2
beverage *(n.)* C1
challenge *(v.)* + OPAL B2
complexity *(n.)* + OPAL C1
eliminate *(v.)* + OPAL B2
encourage *(v.)* + OPAL B1
expert *(n.)* + OPAL A2
finding *(n.)* + OPAL B2
follow through with *(v. phr.)* C1
genetic *(adj.)* + B2
ingest *(v.)* C2
initial *(adj.)* + OPAL B2
link *(n.)* + OPAL A2
metabolize *(v.)* C2
participate *(v.)* + OPAL B1
physical *(adj.)* + OPAL A2
physician *(n.)* + C1
practical *(adj.)* + OPAL B1
promising *(adj.)* + B2
series *(n.)* + OPAL A2

thus *(adv.)* + OPAL B2
variation *(n.)* + OPAL B2

UNIT 6

acquire *(v.)* + OPAL B2
adjust *(v.)* + OPAL B2
ambiguous *(adj.)* C1
analyze *(v.)* + B1
anticipate *(v.)* + B2
approach *(v.)* + B2
collaborative *(adj.)* C1
constant *(adj.)* + OPAL B2
contact *(v.)* + B1
enable *(v.)* + OPAL B2
expertise *(n.)* + OPAL B2
fixed *(adj.)* + B1
incentive *(n.)* + B2
income *(n.)* + B2
institution *(n.)* + B2
interpret *(v.)* + OPAL B2
particular *(adj.)* + OPAL A2
pattern *(n.)* + OPAL A2
permanent *(adj.)* + B2
predictable *(adj.)* + B2
reluctant *(adj.)* + C1
transition *(n.)* + OPAL B2
utilize *(v.)* + OPAL C1

UNIT 7

abundant *(adj.)* C1
accommodate *(v.)* + B2
alliance *(n.)* + C1
ample *(adj.)* C1
controversial *(adj.)* + B2
disperse *(v.)* C1
dread *(v.)* C1
ecological *(adj.)* + OPAL C1
empirical *(adj.)* + OPAL C1
evidence *(n.)* + OPAL A2
expedition *(n.)* + B1
habitat *(n.)* + B2

intervene *(v.)* + OPAL C1
overwhelmingly *(adv.)* C1
preliminary *(adj.)* + C1
propose *(v.)* + OPAL B2
reserves *(n.)* + B2
resilient *(adj.)* C1
reveal *(v.)* + OPAL B2
significant *(adj.)* + OPAL B2
sophisticated *(adj.)* + B2
sufficient *(adj.)* + OPAL B2
sustainable *(adj.)* + B2
unduly *(adv.)* C2

UNIT 8

alleviation *(n.)* C2
attach *(v.)* + B1
charity *(n.)* + A2
convenience *(n.)* + B2
criteria *(n.)* + OPAL B2
cumulative *(adj.)* OPAL C2
faculty *(n.)* + C1
flexible *(adj.)* + OPAL B2
fragile *(adj.)* + C1
incur *(v.)* + C1
induce *(v.)* + OPAL C1
locale *(n.)* C2
methodology *(n.)* + OPAL C1
output *(n.)* + OPAL B2
prevail *(v.)* + C1
ratio *(n.)* + OPAL C1
relevance *(n.)* + OPAL C1
respective *(adj.)* + C1
stabilize *(v.)* + OPAL C1
substantial *(adj.)* + OPAL C1
susceptible *(adj.)* C1
twist *(v.)* + C1
vague *(adj.)* + C1
vibrate *(v.)* C2